Praise for *Strengthened by Grace*

Reading this book, I found valuable insights and I would encourage
everyone to read it.

DR. JAMES A. SCUDDER
Founder/Sr. Pastor, Quentin Road Bible Baptist Church
Victory in Grace Television and Radio
Lake Zurich, IL

Strengthened by Grace: A Systematic Theology Handbook is not a watered
down theology but a boiled down study of the doctrines of God in a
concise and useable format. It is a must read for any student of the "whole
counsel of God."

KEN KILINSKI, Th.M.
Parson to Person, Inc.

Pastor Rich Wager proved to be a person deeply in love with God and His
Word. God came first in Rich's life anywhere and everywhere. His ministry,
teaching, and writings reflect his desire to impact and enrich the lives of
others spiritually in their personal study and daily life.

Our friendship reaches back many years to Silver Birch Ranch in
Wisconsin where I was conducting a week of meetings for his church.
Rich and I found time every day between meetings spending the entire
time just talking about the Lord and God's Word which pulsates with the
life of Christ. Our friendship continued up to and including his pastoral
ministry where he developed his studies to give a deeper understanding
of God's Word.

I believe his handbook on systematic theology for believers will be a
great help as they study scripture.

REV. CHARLES SVOBODA
Founder and Director Emeritus of Bible Related Ministries
Hinsdale, IL

Rich Wager had a passion to equip his people with the Word (Eph 4:15-16). His outlines on systematic theology trained a generation for service and ministry to our Lord. I was one of them, and am deeply grateful for the foundation that these studies laid that is still bearing fruit in my life and ministry.

RON ELWARDT
Associate Pastor of Family Life, Camelback Bible Church
Paradise Valley, Arizona

When seeking truth in preparing leaders for today's institutions of learning, I refer to God's Holy Word. This book is a leader friendly guide to understanding the Biblical way, which is always the hardest way. Richard Wager has eased the journey as he references the Biblical way to finding truth in our personal lives and for those who are developing leadership attributes.

DR. GLENN L. KOONCE
Director of the Educational Leadership Program, Regent University
Virginia Beach, VA

The art and craft of any good theologian and teacher involves the ability to make the complex simple. Pastor Richard Wager accomplishes this enormous task in his systematic theology handbook. After spending several years under Pastor Wager's teaching both as a member of his church and at Silver Birch Ranch, I know for a fact that he believed the Bible could be read and understood by everyone. This handbook is a worthy guide in helping unearth the greatest treasures of wisdom and knowledge of God that will nourish your soul. "Richard Wager's handbook on systematic theology is an excellent and practical source to begin one's study in theology. The subject of systematic theology is so vast that even the advanced learner will find it as a practical guide for reference. I have personally used this handbook over the years and would recommend it to anyone who desires to know God more.

ROY FRUITS, Th.M.
Lead Pastor, Rockpoint Church
Lake Elmo, MN

The most critical issue for Christianity in this 21st century is theological. In times such as these, when absolute answers to life's important questions seem to be few, sound Biblical doctrine is not only a precious commodity but an absolute necessity. Attending church Sunday after Sunday as a young believer, I discovered that Pastor Wager not only profoundly understood and taught sound doctrine, but also lived it out practically and victoriously. This sound Biblical teaching has served as an invaluably essential foundation for my personal growth and service in the Lord Jesus. Here in this book you, too, will also have that opportunity to encounter those same powerful and life-changing Biblical truths as you grow in His grace.

DR. RICHARD HESS
Dean of Students, Nicolet Bible Institute
White Lake, WI

I had the privilege of sitting under the teaching ministry of Pastor Richard Wager for over 14 years. He exegeted many of the books of the Bible and had his notes distributed to the congregation. This little book is the distillation of his teachings systematized. Pastor Wager believed that dispensationalism was the only valid way to understand biblical prophecy. His chapter on eschatology, which is the longest chapter in the book, makes for very interesting reading. This book is largely a collection of brief statements with scriptural references in support of the author's thesis. It isn't a tome on systematic theology, but rather a quick reference book which forces the reader to do the digging into scripture to form his own opinions.

DR. BILL WAGNER
Chairman Missions Committee, Emmanuel Bible Church,
Berwyn, IL

This systematic theology handbook provides a clear cut, no nonsense approach to explaining the doctrines that form the foundation of Christianity. It is the one tool I've returned to time and time again for almost 30 years.

Sharon Busenbark
Businesswoman and homemaker
Granger, IN

Strengthened
by Grace
A Systematic Theology Handbook

Strengthened
by Grace
A Systematic Theology Handbook

Richard E. Wager

GRACE ACRES PRESS

CULTIVATING JOY

Grace Acres Press
P.O. Box 22
Larkspur, CO 80118
888-700-GRACE (4722)
(303) 681-9995
(303) 681-9996 fax
www.GraceAcresPress.com

Grace Acres Press also publishes books in a variety of electronic
formats. Some content that appears in primt may not be available in
electronic books.

ISBN: 978-1-60265-006-0

Printed in the United States of America

10 09 08 07   01 02 03 04 05 06 07 08 09 10

Dedication

This book is dedicated to all the young people who have grown up being taught the truths of God's Word at Silver Birch Ranch, and who have continued to learn, teach, and live in a way that shows the world that God is indeed God. Rich Wager is presently in the very presence of God and has joined the throng of thousands who are cheering you on to the finish.

> **1 Corinthians 15:58:** Therefore, my beloved brethren, be ye steadfast, unmoveable, always abounding in the work of the Lord, forasmuch as ye know that your labor is not in vain in the Lord.

Contents

Foreword

A Remembrance of Rich Wager

The year was 1933; Chicago was celebrating the World's Fair. However, in the midst of these festive city activities, God was planning a ministry that would reach around the world with the precious message of the Gospel. The heartbeat and lifeblood of this ministry was Lance Latham, who was working alongside Paul Rader at the amazing gospel witness called the Chicago Gospel Tabernacle in Chicago. To begin the new ministry, Lance took over an abandoned furniture store that had been ravaged by the Great Chicago Fire. As this two-story building was renovated, the first floor became the sanctuary, and the second floor became a clubroom to attract kids in the neighborhood to the Gospel—these young people were the initial focus of the ministry. Even though I had no formal Christian education training, I was honored to be selected to be the youth director of this challenging new ministry, which was named the North Side Gospel Center.

I remember the first day that Rich Wager, then but a young lad, came to the club for the first time. He came from a home with an alcoholic father, but the excitement and friendliness of the club leadership immediately won his heart. How would one describe Rich Wager? You could say that his batteries were always fully charged; if you rated his enthusiasm on a scale from one to ten, he would get a twelve. He had the mark of leadership from the very beginning: In every activity, he was determined to win; losing just made him more determined to win the next time. Win or lose, he always had an enthusiastic smile that signaled his leadership to his clubber friends.

After he trusted Christ to be his Savior, he grew faster spiritually than any clubber I ever saw. As a teenager, in addition to being a junior leader, he also accepted the burden of conducting his own Sunday school class. God blessed him with teaching skills from the very beginning. What a beautiful sight to watch him mentoring the kids he was teaching!

In 1950, the AWANA program was being developed so that it could be available for other churches to use as a ministry in their neighborhoods. I knew if the program was to grow, God would have to send leadership to make it happen, and God answered prayer by bringing Rich Wager beside me as our very first employee. Together we shared a desk under a stairwell—that was AWANA's first "headquarters" office. Rich directed the eighty-member Pioneer Club at the North Side Gospel Center while I directed the high school club called Pilots. Soon church leaders were coming from everywhere to see the new clubs in action.

Rich and I together acted as a "think tank" as we were challenged to develop the AWANA program. No funds were available, and the test for the clubbers was all we had. Nevertheless, Rich said that we must strive for excellence, and we must get a printing press of our own so that we could print our own books. To raise money for a press, we gathered the clubbers together every Saturday and filled our church bus with newspapers collected from the basements and sheds of many homes. With the proceeds from sale of the scrap papers, we were able to purchase a second-hand printing press. However, neither one of us knew how to run our new machine! Rich, who was very creative, learned first, and together we printed the first book and its covers; the clubbers were corralled to come each afternoon to collate them.

God was blessing AWANA each summer and Camp AWANA was a vital part of our ministry. Rich was one of the key camp leaders, and it was there that God taught us many of the basic principles of running a camp. I believe it was there that God gave Rich the vision and direction to direct camps.

The most discouraging moment of my life was when Rich shared with me that God was calling him to leave the ministry of AWANA. It was like having my right arm severed, but it was obvious that God was leading him. He became youth pastor at Midwest Bible Church, where he soon got the AWANA program going, and before long he came up with the idea of interclub competition, which developed into the AWANA nationwide Olympics. With the camping heart he had, Rich also developed the Phantom Ranch camp ministry. Later he moved on to become the pastor of the Emmanuel Bible Church in Berwyn; by then he was developing Bible teaching materials and an audiotape ministry. Then, the birth of the amazing camp at Silver Birch became a reality.

Rich also had a heart for foreign missions, and was selected to become the chairman of the AWANA Foreign Missions program. He was also a member of the New Tribes Teaching staff, whose members taught all the missionary candidates the basic truths of the Bible and showed them how to share the message of the Gospel.

I can only hint at the joy I had in working alongside one of God's brilliant, yet humble, servants. Lance Latham, founder of the North Side Gospel Center and Camp AWANA, also had a large part in mentoring Rich Wager. In turn, Rich has mentored and touched thousands of lives, and his legacy continues today. What an inspiration and a blessing he was to me! I thank God for sending him across my path in life. He truly was a special friend.

Every believer, every parent, and every church should consider using this book to strengthen and build a biblical foundation of God's grace in the hearts of our present generation. In Colossians 4:17, the apostle Paul challenges every believer to "Take heed to the ministry which thou have received in the Lord that thou fulfill it." Praise God that Rich Wager, God's servant, faithfully fulfilled the ministry to which he had been ordained. Rich truly lived his life verse, 1 Corinthians 15:58: "Be ye steadfast, unmoveable, always abounding in the work of the Lord, forasmuch as ye know that your labor is not in vain in the Lord."

ART RORHEIM
Founder of AWANA Clubs International

Preface

A good friend of mine, who is also a pastor, once said to me, "Those who are busy serving haven't time to write books." I guess that conversation took place when we were commiserating over the subject of our long days and busy hours in the ministry, and perhaps bewailing the fact that some of our study and experience couldn't be shared with anyone other than those to whom we ministered in person.

The truth of the matter is that we are called by the Lord to our ministries. We should each remain faithful to our specific ministry and let the Lord decide if our study notes and outlines are worth distributing to others. So, that is what we are doing: endeavoring to be faithful in the "ministry for the edifying of the body of Christ, till we all come in the unity of the faith, and of the knowledge of the Son of God unto a perfect man, unto the measure of the stature of the fullness of Christ" (Ephesians 4:12-13). These notes are not the result of extreme effort; instead, they are the result of some blessed hours in the Word with the people of Emmanuel Baptist Church in Berwyn, Illinois. At the request of some of those people, we have compiled them in this handbook.

This book contains three years' worth of the notes and outlines used in our Wednesday night "Hour of Power" Bible study at Emmanuel Baptist Church. It is very much an outline of important points that are worthy of much fuller study, and many of the notes are just that: *notes*, intended only to introduce a subject or fact and get you thinking about that area. The contents are both an overview and a condensation of the vital areas of systematic theology, presented (we hope) in simple style and language. We hope that this handbook can become a trustworthy reference for you when you wish to investigate Biblical teachings. It is far from exhaustive, but it does introduce critical subjects and perhaps will encourage you to delve in greater depth into various subjects—

perhaps by starting an in-depth study of the books listed in the bibliography.

May the Lord bless you as you truly become "an approved worker" in the sight of God (2 Timothy 2:15).

RICHARD E. WAGER

Pastor, Emmanuel Baptist Church

Berwyn, Illinois

MALACHI 3:6A (NLT): I AM THE LORD, AND I DO NOT CHANGE.

The more things change, the more they stay the same. The truths found in the Holy Bible are as relevant today as in the day they were written.

When you construct a building you always start with the foundation. Foundations are critical because everything else that attaches to the building will be affected by how precisely the foundation was laid. It is a wise builder who recognizes the foundation's value and invests enough time and energy to ensure the structural integrity for what will rest on that foundation.

Rich Wager loved to build. He spent time building homes, camp buildings, and churches. Most of all, as a local pastor for more than thirty years, he loved laying the foundational bricks of sound doctrine in the lives of young people. While he was alive, Pastor Wager was able to take some of the most powerful truths of the Bible and make them understandable to the young and uneducated—while still attracting to his congregation those who were professors at the nearby Moody Bible Institute.

This book contains an outline of the basic truths, or doctrine of the Christian faith, as understood and taught to Rich's congregation. We hope that you will be able to use this book to learn these truths and somehow read in between the lines and hear how Rich might have made this truth applicable to your everyday life.

It is our hope that, as you read and understand the truths contained in this book, and ultimately in the Book of Books, that you will adjust your life to the truth and not attempt to adjust the truth to your life. We wish you God's best as you begin to build your life on His solid foundation.

Acknowledgments

We would like to thank Joyce (Rich's wife), Rick and Dave Wager, and their families for allowing this book to be published. Grateful thanks also to Roberta Berggren, Rich's faithful secretary, who compiled the original copy of this document, as well as to all those who are a part of Emmanuel Bible Church and Silver Birch Ranch families, for whom this material was originally intended. We also thank Anne Fenske for her vision for Grace Acres Press, and the intentional purpose to publish material that will help build the Kingdom.

Bibliography

The books listed here were the source and foundation of much of the material in this handbook, in addition to personal notes and outlines accumulated through the years in our ministry. We have endeavored to acknowledge each instance in which material was directly quoted from any of these authors. On occasion, material written by others was used in part and adapted by the author of this handbook to emphasize certain doctrinal points and teachings.

Cambron, Mark G. *Bible Doctrines: Beliefs That Matter.* Grand Rapids, Mich.: Zondervan, 1954.

Chafer, Lewis Sperry. *Major Bible Themes* (rev. ed.; John F. Walvoord, ed.). Grand Rapids, Mich.: Zondervan, 1974.

Chafer, Lewis Sperry. *Systematic Theology (vols. 1–6).* Dallas, Tex.: Dallas Seminary Press, 1947–1948.

Koch, Kurt E. *Between Christ and Satan.* Grand Rapids, Mich.: Kregel, 1962).

Pentecost, J. Dwight. *Things to Come.* Findley, Ohio: Dunham Publishing, 1958.

Strong, Augustas Hopkins. *Systematic Theology.* The Judson Press, 1907.

Thayer, Joseph Henry. *Greek-English Lexicon of the New Testament.* N.p., 1962.

Thiessen, Henry C. *Lectures in Systematic Theology.* Grand Rapids, Mich.: William B. Eerdsman Publishing Co., 1949.

Unger, Merrill F. *Demons in the World Today.* Wheaton, Ill.: Tyndale, 1972.

Bible versions used were:

✦ King James Version (Authorized) [abbreviated as KJV]

- New American Standard Bible [abbreviated as NAS]
- American Standard Version [abbreviated as ASV]
- New International Version [abbreviated as NIV]
- Notes from the *Ryrie Study Bible* and the *New Scofield Bible.*

Bibliology
Doctrine of the Bible

☙❧

INTRODUCTION

"Why do you believe the Bible is true?" This question may be asked of any teacher of the Word and of anyone who testifies to another of the great and glorious hope that the Christian possesses. It is a question that every Christian should settle in his or her own heart and be prepared to answer at any time, confronting any challenge that arises to the authenticity and authority of the Word.

We believe that the Bible is more than a book: It is the living, God-breathed Word of God presenting to us all the knowledge concerning God and His relationship to humanity that we need to know. This does *not* mean that other manifestations of God are not present in nature and experience; however, all these other evidences are subordinate to the final and complete revelation that is the Bible in its original language. The written Word tells of the living Word (John 1:1; 2 Timothy 3:16; Hebrews 4:12; 1 Peter 1:23; John 6:63).

That is why in this Bible doctrine course we chose to commence with the theme of Bibliology, or a study of the Bible, stressing the fact that it is an authoritative, authentic message from God.

A so-called believer who does not recognize the authority and importance of the Bible is an unstable person, and a believer who ignores the Bible is carnal and approaches life from a human viewpoint rather than the divine viewpoint. The real reason for studying Bibliology is given in 1 Peter 3:15.

We will now break down Bibliology into systematic divisions for study. We investigate some of the facts concerning the origin of the Bible, as well as its subject and purpose. We note basic, interesting facts concerning the Word and in so doing give reasons why we believe the Bible is true and is a direct communication from God to humans.

I. External Evidence on Why We Believe the Bible Is God's Word

- The miracle of its survival: It is and has been divinely protected. Efforts by Jehoiakim, king of Judah, to destroy God's word failed (Jeremiah 36:21-32). In AD 303, Diocletian instigated the most tremendous onslaught against the Bible the world has known: every manuscript found was destroyed; every family found with a portion of Scripture was martyred. After two years, a column of victory was erected over the ashes of destroyed Bibles with the inscription: "Extinct is the name of Christians." Twenty years later, Constantine, offering a reward, found fifty copies of the Bible in twenty-four hours. Princes of Egypt, Babylon, Persia, and Rome, Alexander the Great, and other world leaders and states have tried to stamp it out, and each effort has failed.

- Its perpetuation: Wycliffe, hated by church and state, persisted in translation of Scripture, and many who helped him were burned. His body was exhumed and burned, but his manuscripts survived. Tyndale was strangled and burned at the stake for the crime of translating and disseminating Scriptures; three years later, the English king authorized its printing. Today the Bible is all over Russia and the former Iron Curtain countries. It survived; the Soviet Union did not.

- Its invulnerability to disbelief: Voltaire allegedly said that in 100 years, the Bible would be a forgotten book. Thomas Paine, in his *Age of Reason* (1795), said that he had completely undercut the Bible's claims to authority and divine authorship. Ingersoll held up a Bible and said, "In fifteen years I will have this book in the morgue." Obviously, they were all wrong.

ᎌ Its influence in the world: It has been translated into and printed in many languages; there are millions of copies and multiple millions of followers; men died to bring it to others; and nations, as well as individual men and women, have changed because of it.

ᎌ Its unity: This collection of 66 books, though written by many authors over 1,600 years, is without contradiction. Different cultures and backgrounds made no difference in the continuity or sequence of subject matter. Creation to New Heaven and Earth; the doctrines of salvation, God, sin, man, and all the rest, are all consistent, as are the types of Christ and infinite subjects.

ᎌ Its supreme claims: No other book claims divine authorship (or no other such claims hold up).

ᎌ Its subject matter: God, creation, prophecy, nature.

ᎌ Its accuracy in science and history.

ᎌ Its place in literature: its importance as a book and cultural influence.

ᎌ Archaeology cries out with proof after proof supporting the manuscript, from the Dead Sea Scrolls to hundreds of archaeological digs in the Eastern world. Examples:
  ᎌ Flood in Babylonian literature—flood tablets found by George Smith, 1872.
  ᎌ Flood deposit at Ur—Woolley, 1929.
  ᎌ Babylon—Ur, Ziggurat, Abraham.
  ᎌ Egypt—pyramids, famine, death of firstborn, plus much more; Rosetta Stone, 1799.

II. INTERNAL EVIDENCE ON
WHY WE BELIEVE THE BIBLE IS GOD'S WORD

- It claims to be the Word of God (Joshua 1:8; Psalms 1:2, 12:6, 19:7-11; Romans 10:17; 1 Corinthians 2:13; Colossians 3:16); the authors claimed no glory for themselves.

- Its prophecy has been fulfilled in minute detail. Examples:
  - Noah's sons.
  - Israel's bondage.
  - Future of Jacob's sons.
  - Israel in the land.
  - John the Baptist.
  - Birth of Christ.
  - Offices and ministries of Christ.
  - Messiah to be Jew (Numbers 24:17, 19):
    - Of tribe of Judah (Genesis 49:10).
    - Of family of David (Psalms 89:3, 4).
    - Born in Bethlehem (Micah 5:2).
    - Raised in Galilee (Isaiah 9:1, 2).
    - Born of a virgin (Isaiah 7:14).
    - Childhood in Egypt (Hosea 11:1, plus many others concerning Christ).
  - Dispersion of the Jews (Deuteronomy 28:63-65).
  - Jews' ceaseless suffering (Deuteronomy 28:25-35, plus others).
  - Egypt—worst of kingdoms (Ezekiel 29:15), plus others on Babylon, Nineveh, Tyre (Isaiah 23:3, 8; Ezekiel 26:5, 14), and many other nations.
  - Four kingdoms of Daniel.

- Supernatural content of Scripture: creation, God, heaven, spirit, etc.

III. SCRIPTURE IS INSPIRED OF GOD

Passages on inspiration: 2 Timothy 3:16; 2 Peter 1:21; Genesis 1:3; among others.

Theories of inspiration include:

- Mechanical or dictation theory—writers were stenographers dictated to by God; problem is vocabulary, style, and writer's personal feelings (Romans 7, 9:1-3; letter closings, etc.).

- Concept theory—weakens inspiration by saying God gave a concept or thought to writers and then left them to express the divine thought in their own words.

- Mystical or partial inspiration—parts are inspired but we cannot accept historical, geographical, and scientific statements as accurate.

- Neo-orthodox—there are errors in Scripture; Scripture is not literally true, but God speaks to us through the Bible anyway (Karl Barth).

- Naturalistic—just men writing; God didn't have anything to do with the writing.

- Verbal—plenary; God guided and inspired spirit-filled men to write in their own language and style, but God watched choice of words and guarded the message to keep it accurate; human authors inspired by God.

IV. THE BIBLE IS DIVINE REVELATION

- It is reasonable to assume that God would reveal Himself to the highest of his created creatures.

- Three forms of revelation:
  - Creation (Psalms 19; Romans 1:20)—limited; no holiness of love, but power and wisdom; heathen will be judged for not worshipping God.
  - Christ (John 1)—revealed God's plan, love, and grace.
  - Written Word—Bible understood only through special illumination by the Spirit (1 Corinthians 2:10-14). This eliminates the problem of correct interpretation. It completes the purpose and plan of God: an even greater revelation. Now Spirit through Word illuminates and guides, but rules of interpretation must be followed.

▸ The Bible is a unique book and the only one authoritatively accepted as God's original revelation of Himself to humankind. Key word is *authority*.

V. CHRIST'S TESTIMONY CONCERNING THE VALIDITY OF SCRIPTURE

Matthew 5:18; John 10:35; Matthew 1:22, 23, 4:14, 8:17.

▸ Christ predicted the writing of the New Testament (John 16:12, 13; Matthew 28:19).

▸ Don't forget that sometimes the Bible accurately records a lie as a lie: Genesis 3:4 and the book of Ecclesiastes are man's philosophy. Apparent contradictions are always explained and resolved with careful study.

VI. THE BIBLE'S SUBJECT AND PURPOSE

Subject—Jesus Christ

▸ Creator—Elohim (plural) (John 1:3; Colossians 1:16, 17; Hebrews 1:2, 3).

▸ Supreme ruler of world (Psalms 2:8, 9; Romans 14:11; Philippians 2:9-11; Revelation 19:15, 16).

▸ King of Israel (Luke 1:31-33).

▸ Judge of all men (John 5:27; Isaiah 9:6, 7; Psalms 72).

▸ The Incarnate Word—God embodied (John 1:1; Hebrews 1:3).

▸ Savior of the world—promised seed (Genesis 3:15); will bear sins of world (Isaiah 53:4-6; John 1:29); only Savior (Acts 4:12; 1 Corinthians 15:3, 4; 2 Corinthians 5:19-21).

Purpose—Manifestation of Glory of God

▸ Angels were created and material universe designed to reflect God's glory. Man created in likeness of God. God is worthy of infinite respect and glory, and the revelation of God to His creatures has provided them with a worthy object of love and devotion and given them ground for faith and peace of mind. Verses that show supreme importance:

- ❧ Israel for God's glory (Colossians 1:16; Psalm 19:1).
- ❧ Salvation is glory to God (Isaiah 43:7, 21, 25; Romans 9:23; Ephesians 2:7, 3:10).
- ❧ Service is for God's glory (Matthew 5:16; John 15:8; 1 Corinthians 10:31; 2 Timothy 3:16, 17).
- ❧ We desire God glorified (Romans 5:2).
- ❧ Believer's death glorifies God (John 21:19; Philippians 1:20).
- ❧ We are to share Christ's glory (John 17:22; Colossians 3:4).

VII. HOW THE BIBLE CAME TO US

Old Testament

- ❧ The Old Testament was written over 1,000 years (1450 BC to 400 BC) on leather or papyrus (*paper*). Papyrus is an ancient plant that grew in Galilee and Nile (now Sudan), and was used to make paper as early as 2800 BC. It was soaked and then the fibers were laid horizontally and vertically with an adhesive; the fixed fibers were then pressed and dried. The Old Testament was written in old Hebrew prong-shaped archaic letters, which later developed into the round-bellied letters found in the Dead Sea Scrolls and in present Hebrew Bibles.

- ❧ The Old Testament became canonized over a period of time. As the books were written, God impressed upon writers and recipients the books' "God-breathed" (*inspired*) authority and preserved and collected them by miraculously intervening through human interest and care.

- ❧ The Old Testament was translated into the Koine Greek (common language of Christ's day), into a version called the Septuagint, around the years 280–150 BC.

- ❧ The Masoretes (Jews in a certain conservative sect from about AD 600 to AD 950) invented a system of vowels and accents to punctuate and standardize the text, thus providentially preparing it for the printing press 500 years later.

New Testament

- ✦ For twenty years after the ascension of Christ, the Greek Old Testament scriptures (Septuagint) constituted the Bible; then James wrote his epistle (45 AD) and the New Testament was written through the years until John wrote Revelation about 90 AD. During this period, much preaching was from the Old Testament (Peter—Acts 2:14-36; Stephen—Acts 7:2-53; etc.).

- ✦ The New Testament became canonized by the evident leading of the Lord in their preservation and compilation. Criteria for determining validity of a book:
  - ✦ Apostolicity—Was the writer a bona fide apostle? If not, did the author have close association with apostles and their blessings on the work? Many books were thus eliminated, such as Apocalypse, Acts of Paul, Epistle of Barnabas, others that were obviously spurious.
  - ✦ Content—Did the book have spiritual stamp, high order and presentation? Example: Childhood of Jesus was foolishly presented in some books and obviously of low content and spurious.
  - ✦ Universality—Did the early church as a whole receive and accept the book?
  - ✦ Divine inspiration—Did the book show unmistakable evidence of being authored by God? Was it consistent with other Scriptures? Did the Holy Spirit give conviction to the hearts of compilers? Without providential interposition, the New Testament canon would never have come to us.

- ✦ Reasons for doubting certain apocryphal books were that they were actually proven spurious or uninspired and inconsistent with known and accepted inspired books.

- ✦ Growth of canon came through first- and second-century scholars such as Clement of Rome (AD 96), Hermas (AD 150), Irenaeus, Tertullian, Cyppian, etc.; then through later scholars such as Jerome, Augustine, church councils, etc. By AD 200, the Bible contained essentially the same books we have today. The Roman church, at the Council of Trent in

1546, declared eleven of the fourteen apocryphal books canonical. We do not accept these books, for the above stated reasons:

- 1 Ezdras—Same historical material found in Ezra, Nehemiah, and 2 Chronicles. However, contains a legendary story of three Jewish pages in Darius's court to ascertain wisdom; winner Zerubbabel claimed as his prize permission for Jews to return and build Jerusalem.
- 2 Ezdras—Composite of prophecies, visions, legends.
- Tobit—Religious fiction.
- Judith—Fictional narrative with didactic value.
- Remainder of Esther—Greek addition to book of Esther.
- Wisdom of Solomon—Most attractive and interesting of apocryphal books, although latter part is inferior to first two sections.
- Ecclesiasticus—Only one whose author we know (Jesus, son of Sirach of Jerusalem, 175 BC); one of the better apocryphal books.
- 1 Maccabees—Historical and literary book of high quality; contains some false doctrine but is looked upon as historically correct.
- 2 Maccabees (175–160 BC)—Same period as 1 Maccabees but inferior as to historical worth; myths.
- Baruch—Supposedly written by Jeremiah's secretary.
- Song of three children—Apocryphal addition to Daniel.
- Story of Susanna—Apocryphal addition to Daniel.
- Bel and the Dragon—Legend designed to ridicule idolatry; third addition to Daniel.
- Prayers of Manasses—Purported penitential prayer of a wicked king of Judah.

Pseudepigrapha and Other Religious Writings

There are many other religious writings of the period 200 BC to AD 200 (for example, Assumption of Moses, Ascension of Isaiah, Book of Enoch, Book of Jubilees, etc.), but these have been rejected even by Roman Catholics as being part of divinely inspired Scripture.

Six reasons why apocryphal writings are excluded from the Bible:

- ❧ Never a part of Hebrew Old Testament, which was first Bible of Christian churches.
- ❧ Christ never quoted from or referred to any apocryphal book.
- ❧ New Testament makes not a single reference to or ever quotes from these writings.
- ❧ Though some held in high literary esteem, none approach quality of inspired writings.
- ❧ Authorship dubious and sometimes misrepresented.
- ❧ Unity and harmony of Scripture disrupted.

Other Religious Writings

- ❧ *Talmud* (teaching)—Body of Hebrew civil and canonical laws based on the Torah of Moses; condensation of rabbinical thinking from 300 BC to AD 500. It consists of:
  - ❧ *Mishnah*—Traditional or oral law deduced from written law of Moses.
  - ❧ *Gemara*—A commentary written in Aramaic on legal traditions.

VIII. HOW WE DEAL WITH SO-CALLED ERRORS OF SCRIPTURE

First, we do not admit to any error in Scripture, that is, the original manuscripts. We know that all apparent discrepancies found in Scripture can be explained.

Allegers of Biblical error base their objections in the areas of science, history, morality, reasoning, interpretation of Old Testament, prophecy, and general content, such as objections to miracles, dispute over godly attributes, and that which is contrary to human senses and/or not possible to test and determine.

Answers lie in many areas, such as:

- In science:
  - Human authors oftentimes didn't know or use scientific terms. We often refer to "sunset" and "sunrise," even though we now know the earth rotates rather than sun moving. Imagery such as "the sun stood still," "world cannot be moved," "four corners of the earth" are obviously common-life phrases rather than scientific terms.
  - It can safely be said that science has not yet proven any Scripture passage untrue.
- In history:
  - Answer often lies in use of rounded numbers; for example, Numbers 25:9 (24,000) versus 1 Corinthians 10:8 (23,000)—probably number was in between.
  - Various apparent discrepancies in values are explained by differences among Roman, Greek, and Babylonian measurements; for example, a "talent" in one system may differ greatly from a "talent" in another.
  - Various calendars, ethnic backgrounds, terminology, use of numbers easily explain some discrepancies; for example, Paul's use of 430 years (Galatians 3:17) is a quote from the Septuagint, which he was using for the people he was teaching. The issue then was not years but a more important truth; for him to use the Hebrew 600 years rather than the Hellenist 430 would have confused the men he was writing to.
  - Sometimes an apparent discrepancy would be explained if we knew one more fact. For example, one blind man or two—Matthew 20:30 and Luke 18:35—could be understood in light of going and coming from Jericho.
- In morality:
  - Rahab's duplicity rather than faith is criticized. Answer—a baby believer (spiritual child) does not grasp what a mature believer will in time come to understand.

- God's righteous sovereignty seems unjust to the "natural" mind.
- Evil acts of good men (e.g., Noah's drunkenness, Lot's incest, David's misdeeds, etc.) are not sanctioned by God; they are simply recorded.
- Some acts are relatively just (e.g., destruction of Canaanite tribes).

- In differences between Old Testament and New Testament:
  - Oftentimes New Testament writer had further revelation.
  - Old Testament partially quoted because of dispensation truths.
  - Septuagint Bible used as accommodation; didn't impair teaching truth.

- In apparent errors in prophecy:
  - Some prophecies not fulfilled yet.
  - Later prophecy explains apparent discrepancy (1 Thessalonians 2:2-5 says "day is now present" ... but later on states "it will not be until falling away")—whole context must be used.
  - Character of prophecy is highly figurative, so some make errors in interpretation.

Theology
Doctrine of God

❧

INTRODUCTION

Obviously, this section is far from exhaustive. Hundreds of books have been written about God and on various themes concerning the nature of God Himself, His work, His personality, and so on. However, the greatest source book is the Bible itself: A person desiring to know God should recognize that one really can get to know the Lord best through study of the Bible, which is the total and absolute revelation from God and about God.

Did you ever consider reading the Bible through with a single theme in mind? How about this theme: to find out all you can about God Himself. Forget the great men, miracles, great themes, and doctrine; just read to familiarize yourself with God. You might be surprised at the consistent revelation about God Himself.

We will endeavor to identify, in a systematic way, the nature, attributes, and work of God, as well as some false and true systems of theology. But first, a definition.

The word *theology* comes from the Greek word *theos*, meaning God; thus, *theology* is the study of God; more specifically, the doctrine of God. To begin a study of Bible doctrine, we must begin with the source of all things: God (Genesis 1:1; John 1:1; Hebrews 1:1). We must also assume that God has made available to us all the knowledge we need about Him, for, as we shall see later, He is just in His dealings with humans as well as loving and omniscient.

He never makes mistakes, and though He expects humans to respond to Him, He will always be fair in judging humanity.

Many questions arise about the nature of God. Who is He? What is He? What is His relationship to humankind? Or, more specifically, what has He to do with me? We would first like to look at God and divide these thoughts into two areas: (1) the essence (substance) of God, and (2) His attributes (nature). We could also say this as (1) what is He made of and (2) what is He like?

I. ESSENCE: THE SUBSTANCE OF GOD

God is spiritual (John 4:24). Though God is made of substance, it is a spiritual rather than material substance. This is hard for us to understand, but we believe this and it is consistent with other revelations of God. The article is not used in John 4:24: It does not say that God is "*a* spirit" but that God is spirit. He is present everywhere. This suggests the following truths:

- ❧ God is immaterial (not made of material things) and incorporeal (read Luke 24:39). This, of course, does not mean that God, while teaching us, does not use symbolic bodily parts to teach us finite humans infinite truths (Hebrews 1:10; Genesis 3:8; 1 Kings 8:29; Psalms 34:15). This is called *anthropomorphism*.

- ❧ God is invisible (John 1:18; Romans 1:20; 1 Timothy 6:16), but believers will someday see Him with glorified eyes (Psalms 17:15; Matthew 5:8; Hebrews 12:14; Revelation 22:4). Those passages of Scripture in which men see God (such as Genesis 32:30; Exodus 3:6, 24:9, 10; and Isaiah 6:1) describe a reflection of His glory, screened off to save man from destruction (as we see in Exodus 33:18-23). All appearances of God in Scripture are either Christ as "the angel of Jehovah" (Genesis 16:7-14, 22:11-18, 31:11-13; Exodus 3:2-6; Daniel 3:25) or as the Holy Spirit in a visible form (John 1:32; Hebrews 1:7). God has never revealed Himself to man in His fullest glory, for such manifestation would destroy man (Exodus 33:20).

- ❧ God is alive. This implies feeling, power, and activity (Joshua

3:10; 1 Samuel 17:26; Psalms 84:2). He is contrasted with dead idols in Psalms 115:3-9.

- God is a person, not an impersonal spirit. The only way to determine what "spirit" is like apart from Scripture is by the analogy of our own spirit. We are personal or have personality, which is self-consciousness and self-determination. We relate feelings and appetites to ourselves. In contrast, an animal—a brute beast—is mechanical. We have choice as to motives, actions, and ends. If we do, how much more God?

- God is self-existent. He is the First Cause, uncaused (Aquinas). He is not dependent, as we are, on anything outside of Himself to exist. It is His nature, not His will, for He cannot annihilate Himself. His name, Jehovah (Exodus 3:14), says this.

- God is infinite, not limited by space. He is greater than finite space and is present everywhere in complete wholeness (1 Kings 8:27; 2 Chronicles 2:6; Jeremiah 23:24; Acts 17:28).

- God is eternal, not limited by time. He is free from the succession of time and the cause of time (Psalms 90:2, 102:27; 1 Timothy 6:18).

II. ATTRIBUTES: THE NATURE OF GOD

To be a bit technical, we will call an *attribute* that which describes the substance (or essence) of God. Some attributes are considered nonmoral and others moral. The following list is not exhaustive.

Nonmoral Attributes

- Omnipresence—present everywhere (Psalms 139:7-12; Acts 17:27, 28). A real comfort to believers.

- Omniscience—all knowledge in past, present, and future (Psalms 139:1-10; Hebrews 4:13; Matthew 10:30).

- Omnipotence—all powerful, able to do what He wills (Genesis 17:1; Job 42:2; Revelation 19:6). *El Shaddai*—

enriches and makes fruitful. Name prior to law (Exodus 6 on) is *Jehovah*.

- Immutability—unchangeable in will, essence, attributes, and consciousness (James 1:17; Malachi 3:6). Immutability doesn't mean that God does not act, for Scripture clearly teaches both. God acts within His prescribed perfect plan. When He repents in Scripture, it is judiciously in response to changeable creatures, but He remains immutable in His justice. He is not like a rock but like mercury in a thermometer: always mercury, but acting and reacting correctly regarding humankind.

Moral Attributes

- Holiness—perfect, sinless, moral. Separated from creatures and sin. Holiness is the foremost attribute and ranks above other attributes, as all others are related to it. God wants to be known as holy above all else (Leviticus 11:44, 45). Examples: Mt. Sinai and the lawgiving; divisions of tabernacle and temple into holy places, many offerings before Israelites could approach God, etc. Teaches three things:
  - There is a chasm between God and the sinner (Isaiah 59:1, 2).
  - Humans must approach God through the merits of another (Romans 5:2; Ephesians 5:18).
  - We should approach God with reverence and godly fear (Hebrews 12:28, 29).
- Righteousness and justice—aspect of holiness in which God deals with the creature (John 17:25; 2 Timothy 4:8). He is right in administration of rewards and punishment.
- Goodness—which includes:
  - God's love, by which He is moved to communicate Himself (2 Corinthians 2:13, 14).
  - God's benevolence and mercy, whereby He manifests affection to creatures; He offers hope to the rejected.

- Grace—offers love and salvation to the undeserving (Romans 2:4, 5, 3:25, 9:22).
- Truth—the only absolute truth. This means that God's revelations, declarations, and representations are always consistent with eternal reality (John 17:3; 1 John 5:10; Romans 3:4).
- Sovereignty—God is supreme over all. He does what He wants to do and what He does is always right. He yields to no other power, authority, or glory.

Figure 1 is an "association sentence" (a mnemonic device) that we devised to help you memorize some of the main attributes of God:

FIGURE 1

Only	Jesus	Our	Righteous	Savior	Loves	Every	Individual	Vanquished	One
m	u	m	i	o	o	t	m	e	m
n	s	n	g	v	v	e	m	r	n
i	t	i	h	e	e	r	u	a	i
p	i	s	t	r		n	t	c	p
o	c	c	e	e		a	a	i	r
t	e	i	o	i		l	b	t	e
e		e	u	g		n	i	y	s
n		n	s	n		e	l		e
c		c	n	t		s	i		n
e		e	e	y		s	t		c
			s				y		e
			s						

III. THE UNITY AND DIVINE TRINITY OF GOD

Our minds cannot grasp this truth, but we believe it because God says it is true. This proves yet again that the Bible is God's Word, for man wouldn't even venture to suggest such an irrational truth as unity and trinity. The Bible teaches both God unity and God trinity.

Unity

Unity (Exodus 20:3; Deuteronomy 6:4; Isaiah 44:6; John 10:30, 14:9, 17:11) means there is one God. Scripture teaches that God is the *only one*, not one of many, and that the divine nature is singular. Both Old and New Testaments refer to God in the plural, probably because of Israel's tendency to idolatry and the Greeks' to polytheism. God is one and God is the only God.

Trinity

Trinity is a truth of revelation, not discoverable by human reasoning. It means that there are three eternal distinctions in the one divine essence, known respectively as Father, Son, and Holy Spirit. They are three persons but one God.

This is not tritheism (three distinct gods). Nor is it saballianism, a third-century idea which held that there was trinity of revelation but not of nature—that is, God just changed forms to perform in various offices. This is error.

God is the same God incarnate who fulfills the offices of Redeemer and Holy Spirit. Trinity is a great mystery, but is the result of revelation, not speculation. We believe because:

- Plural nouns and pronouns are used in Old Testament (*Elohim*) (Genesis 1:1, 2, 3:22, 11:6, 7, among others).

- Jehovah distinguished from Jehovah (Genesis 19:24; Hosea 1:7; 2 Timothy 1:18).

- Jehovah has a son (Psalms 2:7; John 9:35; Romans 1:4; John 3:16, 18).

- Spirit distinguished from God (Genesis 1:1, 2, 6:3).

- The triad of expression (Isaiah 6:3; Numbers 6:24-26).

- The appearances of the angel of the Lord (Hagar, Abraham, Jacob, Moses, among others).

- Baptism of Christ—the Father speaks, the Spirit descends upon Christ.

- Jesus prays to the Father for comfort (John 14:16, 17).

- Baptismal formula (Matthew 28:19, among many others).

Each member of the Trinity has all the divine attributes, though Christ laid some aside in His earthly ministry (Philippians 2:7, 8) or at least surrendered independent exercise of them (Mark 13:32, 11:17, 6:6).

IV. THE NAMES OF GOD

The names of God denote God's character (Psalms 9:10). In the Old Testament there are three principal names:

- Jehovah or Yahweh—first appears in Genesis 2:4; meaning described in Exodus 3:13, 14. Means that God is self-existent, eternal God.

- Elohim—most common Old Testament name (2,300 times), found first in Genesis 1:1. Meaning is debated. It is a plural form and includes the idea of strength; literally means "putter-forth of power."

- Adonai—Master, Lord (Genesis 15:2).

There are many pluralistic names, using combinations of the preceding names or other combinations:

- Jehovah-Jirah—"The Lord will provide" (Genesis 22:14); offering of Isaac.

- Jehovah-Rapha—"The Lord that healeth" (Exodus 15:26); bitter waters of Marah.

- Jehovah-Nissi—"The Lord our banner" (Exodus 17:15); conflict with Amalek.

- Jehovah-Qadash—"The Lord doth sanctify" (Leviticus 20:8); human sacrifices to Moluch.

- Jehovah-Shalom—"The Lord our peace" (Judges 6:24); Gideon.

- Jehovah-Tsidkenu—"The Lord our righteousness" (Jeremiah 23:6); Millennium.

- Jehovah-Shammoth—"The Lord is present" (Ezekiel 48:35); Ezekiel's description of heaven.

- Jehovah-Sabaoth—"The Lord of hosts" (Exodus 12:41); Egyptian bondage lifted.

Others include eloistic combinations: "El Shaddai"—almighty God (Genesis 17:1); "Elelyon"—most high God (Genesis 14:8); "El-Olam"—everlasting God (Genesis 21:33).

In the New Testament we find additional names, such as Father, Son, and Holy Spirit.

V. THE DECREE OF GOD

The sovereign purpose of God is defined theologically as the *decree* of God. The decree of God includes all that God accomplishes through natural law, all events and actions that God does Himself, and all acts of humans. Though we cannot understand it, God has come up with a system whereby He has given humans freedom of choice—yet this all-wise God, in complete knowledge of what humanity will do, has come up with a perfect, divine plan.

The divine plan includes all that has happened, such as Adam and Eve being permitted to sin so that there could be the divine remedy of Christ's death and the work of the Holy Spirit in convincing men of their need. It includes the end of the present heavens and earth and the eternal fellowship of believers with God. It includes all enemies of God being made the footstool of Christ and their eternal rejection.

"It is not a blind, mechanical philosophy of fatalism but an intelligent, loving wise plan in which man, responsible for his choices, is held accountable for what he does and is rewarded for his good work. Before such a God man can only bow in submission, love and adoration" (Chafer, 1947, vol. 1).

VI. FALSE AND TRUE SYSTEMS OF THEOLOGY

- Deism—a God exists that created the earth, but God does not sustain the creation. He is the maker but not the keeper.

- Atheism—there is no God.

- Skepticism—doubt and disbelief with regard to God.

- Agnosticism—God cannot be known, though He may exist.

- Polytheism—there are many gods and/or plateaus and ranks of gods.

⚜ Tritheism—there are three gods.

⚜ Dualism—there are two gods, one good and one bad.

⚜ Theism—belief in a personal God; to be saved, one must go further and accept Him.

⚜ Monotheism—there is one God. We are monotheists, as are Jews, Muslims, and others. This belief alone is not sufficient (James 2:10); however, salvation is (Romans 10:9).

VII. EVIDENCES OF THE EXISTENCE OF GOD

⚜ Cosmological argument—argument from change in nature. Everything begun owes its existence to some producing cause.

⚜ Teleological argument—argument from order and design.

⚜ Anthropological argument—argument from man's mental and moral nature. Humanity must have had an author.

⚜ Ontological argument—argument from abstract and necessary ideas. Our concepts of infinity and eternity presume the existence of an infinite and eternal being.

⚜ Intuitional argument—believe that there must be a God without initial revelation.

⚜ Scriptural revelation.

⚜ Bible presupposes an author.

⚜ Christ's claim to be God. If He was not, who was He?

⚜ Prophecy—only God could know the future.

VIII. FATHERHOOD OF GOD

With the doctrine of trinity, the fatherhood of God is important. God, the first person of the Trinity, is electing, loving, and bestowing; Christ suffers, redeems, and upholds the universe; the Holy Spirit regenerates, indwells, baptizes, energizes, and sanctifies.

The first person is the Father:

⚜ Over creation (Ephesians 3:14, 15; James 1:17).

❧ Of Christ (Ephesians 1:3; Psalms 2:7; John 1:14).

❧ Of believers (John 1:12; Galatians 3:26;
  Ephesians 2:19, 3:15).

Christology
Doctrine of Christ

⁂

INTRODUCTION

The two doctrines of Christology (concerning the person of Christ) and soteriology (concerning the doctrine of salvation) are so closely linked that many theologians deal with them as one. We prefer, however, to treat each of these doctrines separately and thereby emphasize special truths that can be discerned and isolated.

Lest this study become sterile, let's be very careful to remember that this study is to encompass the sweetest character of the eternities. We will sift out facts about Christ, but each fact should only add to your knowledge of the lovely character of the Son of God who loved us and gave Himself for us. There will be many times in the course of this study, I'm sure, when tears will come to the eyes of the instructor and ecstasy into the hearts of student and teacher alike. There will be some preaching and rejoicing along with the investigation of the facts, for we study to "know Christ" and to know Him is to rejoice in the believer's position as bride, brother, and part of the very body of Christ—by His grace. So, keep in mind this purpose: "To know Christ" (Philippians 3:10).

May we join in with Charles Wesley and truly sing from our hearts as we study Christ:

> O for a thousand tongues to sing
> My great Redeemer's praise,

The glories of my God and King,
The triumphs of His grace.

My gracious Master and my God,
Assist me to proclaim,
To spread thro' all the earth abroad,
The honors of Thy name.

Jesus, the name that charms our fears,
That bids our sorrows cease,
'Tis music in the sinner's ears,
'Tis life, and health, and peace.

He breaks the pow'r of canceled sin,
He sets the pris'ner free,
His blood can make the foulest clean,
His blood availed for me.

Hear Him, ye deaf; His praise, ye dumb,
Your loosened tongues employ;
Ye blind, behold your Saviour come;
And leap, ye lame, for joy.

What a mind-boggling study this can be: to study a majesty who was spit on by men, a Creator who became a servant, a Savior who offers eternal life that is rejected by stupid humanity. How ignorant humanity is! Let us study to see who Christ is—and remember always that He is the central theme of the Bible and of everything.

Here is the general outline of this section:

The preincarnate (before birth) Christ
The incarnate Christ (Christ as man)
    His birth and childhood
    Important human incidents
      Baptism
      Temptation
      Transfiguration

Major teachings and discourses
Death
Resurrection
Ascension
Future plans or exaltation of Christ
Special teachings emphasized in the person and work of
Christ
    Historical views of the person of Christ
    Two natures of Christ and the union thereof
    Names and titles of Christ

I. CHRIST PREINCARNATE

What was Christ like? What did He do before His birth on earth through the Virgin Mary? This discussion centers on the eternity and deity of Christ.

- Christ was preexistent and is eternal. Direct statements are found in John 1:1, 2; Micah 5:2; Isaiah 7:14 (Immanuel—God with us); Isaiah 9:6, 7 (the mighty God); John 8:58, 13:3; Colossians 1:15-19; Hebrews1:2, 3, 13:8; Ephesians 1:4; Revelation 1:11.

- Implicatory teachings on preexistence and eternity of Christ:
  - Creation ascribed to Christ (Colossians 1:16; Hebrews 1:10).
  - Angel of Jehovah of Old Testament (theophany) is Christ (Hagar—Genesis 16:7; Jacob—Genesis 48:15, 16; Abraham—Genesis 17:1, 18:1: 22:11-22; Joshua—Judges 2:1-4).

- Names of Christ—see section VI.

- His attributes (John 1:4, 5:26, 14:6; Hebrews 1:11, 7:26, 13:8).

- He is worshipped as God (Hebrews 1:6; John 20:28, among others).

- Christ is Deity (many verses).

Work of Christ in Preincarnate State

- Creator (Romans 11:36; Colossians 1:15-19; Hebrews 1:2-12).

- ✤ Planned world and expression of God's love to man with Trinity before "foundations of world" were laid (Psalms 102:24-27).

- ✤ Appeared in Old Testament, as angel of Jehovah, for direction, comfort, and exhortation.

II. THE INCARNATE CHRIST

Information about the human expression of Christ covers two-fifths of the New Testament.

Reasons for Incarnation

- ✤ To confirm God's promises, from Genesis 3:15 on.

- ✤ To show mercy for gentiles (Romans 15:8, 9).

- ✤ To reveal the Father (John 1:18, 14:9, 16:27).

- ✤ To become a faithful high priest (Hebrews 5:1-5, 4:15, 16).

- ✤ To put away sin (Hebrews 9:26b; Mark 10:45; Leviticus 16:20-22).

- ✤ To destroy the works of the devil (1 John 3:8; Hebrews 2:14, 15).

- ✤ To give us the example of a holy life (Matthew 11:29; 1 John 2:6; 1 Peter 2:21).

- ✤ To prepare for the second advent (Hebrews 9:28; Romans 8:18-25; Revelation 5:6).

Nature of Incarnation

- ✤ He emptied Himself (Philippians 2:7). He did not actually lose His relative attributes (omniscience, omnipotence, and omnipresence), for Christ really retained them (John 2:24, 25, 18:4 (omniscience); John 14:11, 6:36, 10:25, 37, 38, 15:24 (omnipotence); John 3:13 (omnipresence—aware of what happened elsewhere); rather, He surrendered the independent exercise of some of these transitive attributes.

- ✤ He was made into the likeness of men (Philippians 2:7).

His Birth and Childhood

- Purposed before foundation of world (Ephesians 1:4-7, 3:11; Revelation 13:8).

- Anticipated in Old Testament.

- References to lamb, sacrifice, and blood refer to Christ; also, many other types of anticipation, from furniture in tabernacle to individuals such as Joseph, Moses, David.

- Prophecy clearly refers to Christ's coming (Isaiah 9:6, etc.).

- His birth reveals the fact of His humanity (Luke 1:31-35 and 2), but also His divinity, conceived of the Holy Spirit and born of a virgin. So He becomes the:
  - Son of God—divine sonship.
  - Son of man—human.
  - Son of Mary—racial.
  - Son of David—Messianic.
  - Son of Abraham—redemptive.

- As a child, we see the sinless child preparing Himself for His ministry: "I must be about my father's business" (Luke 2:49).

Incidents in His Human Life

- Baptism of Christ—consecration by God to office of priest—Spirit descends and voice acknowledges (Matthew 3:13-17; Mark 1:9-11; Luke 3:21, 22).

- Temptation of Christ—Satan's crucial attack against humanity of Christ is defeated and Christ exhibits to finite minds that their Savior is sinless (Matthew 4:1-11; Mark 1:12, 13; Luke 4:1-13).

- Transfiguration of Christ (Matthew 16:28; Mark 9:1; Luke 9:27)—a setting forth of the power and coming of Christ in His kingdom. It pictures the glory of the coming kingdom; at this time in His ministry, Christ was about to turn from the kingdom ministry to the message of His death and resurrection whereby people who believe will be saved.

Teachings of Christ—Four Main Messages

- Sermon on the Mount—addressed to Israel; message concerning principles and conduct in the kingdom. With the rejection of Christ, complete fulfillment becomes postponed until the kingdom age. Principles of God's dealing with man are applicable to us also (Matthew 5–7).
- Parable of the Sower (Matthew 13)—establishment of church age and principles thereof.
- The Olivet Discourse (Matthew 24, 25)—addressed to Israel and dealing with the end times.
- The Upper Room Discourse (John 13–17)—a discourse which, though given to the disciples, is addressed to the church and the present age. It is the seed plot for all grace teachings, and uncomplicated Christian doctrine is clear in this passage.

Sufferings and Death of Christ

- Sufferings (John 19:28)—actual bearing of sin fell on Christ in His hours of suffering prior to death.
- His death—efficacious sacrifice which is the antithesis of every typical sacrifice; totally responsible for God accepting any sinner and is confirmed as necessary by Old Testament verses, prophecies, and declarations in the synoptic gospels, as well as the writings of John, Paul, Peter, and Hebrews.
- Who put Christ to death? He was:
  - Offered by the Father (John 3:16).
  - Sacrificed of His own free will (John 10:17).
  - Sacrificed by the Spirit (Hebrews 9:14).
  - Killed by men—Herod, Pilate, etc. (Acts 2:23).
  - Sacrificed to defeat Satan (Genesis 3:15).
- What Christ's death accomplishes:
  - Assures us of the love of God toward the sinner.
  - Assures a righteous God that His holy demand for just payment for sin is accomplished in the innocent death of

Christ (Romans 4:25; 2 Corinthians 5:21; Galatians 1:4; Hebrews 9:28). He paid the price of our ransom.

- Assures us that Christ's obedience to the law which we have broken functions as an act of propitiation or satisfaction of all of God's righteous demands on the sinner (Hebrews 9:5; Leviticus 16:14; 1 John 2:2, 4:10; Romans 3:25, 26).

- Assures us that we are not only redeemed pt. B and propitiated pt. C, but provided a basis by which the world is reconciled to God (Romans 5:10, 11, 11:15; 1 Corinthians 7:11; 2 Corinthians 5:18-20); thus assures us that we are reconciled and there is no hindrance or restraint in our relationship to God (Romans 5:1).

- Christ became the substitute bearing our penalty (Leviticus 16:21; Isaiah 53:6; Romans 5:6-8; 1 Peter 3:18). By His burial, as scapegoat He carried away the burden of sin.

III. RESURRECTION

The resurrection of the Son of God is an event possibly more fully proven than any other event of history. In the Old Testament, we see predictions and prophecies of Christ's resurrection; in the New Testament, Christ Himself predicts it often. Then there are the historical records contained in the gospels and in the epistles, which give details and verification of Christ's resurrection and postresurrection appearances.

Proofs of Resurrection (1 Corinthians 15)

- At least seventeen postresurrection appearances.

- Empty tomb.

- Witnesses to resurrection were not gullible or easily swayed; demanded proof. Once convinced, they were willing to die to preserve and propagate that truth. Lives changed drastically.

- Holy Spirit gave power to those preaching the resurrection message.

- ॐ Testimony of early church—Lord's supper.

- ॐ Raised by Father (Psalms 16:10; Acts 2:27, 31, 32; Romans 6:4; Ephesians 1:19, 20), and by the Son Himself (John 2:19, 10:17, 18), and by the Spirit (1 Peter 3:18).

- ॐ The death of Christ pays for sin, but the resurrection verifies Christ's power and authority to pay for sin and establishes a new Headship over a perfected new creation.

Importance of Resurrection and Reasons for Resurrection

- ॐ Because of who He is, it is impossible to capture and hold the "Son of God" imprisoned in death (Acts 2:24; Romans 1:3, 4).

- ॐ Arose to be head over all things (Ephesians 1:22, 23), including the church.

- ॐ Arose to defeat death and bestow resurrection on all who believe (John 12:24; 1 Corinthians 15).

- ॐ Arose because His work of justification was completed (Romans 4:25).

- ॐ Arose as a pattern (first fruit) for all believers (1 Corinthians 15:20-23; Philippians 3:20, 21; 1 Timothy 6:16).

- ॐ Arose to sit on David's throne and thus fulfill all covenant promises to Israel (Acts 2:30).

IV. ASCENSION

Resurrection and ascension are Christ being exalted to His great priestly ministry for believers. In this study we are referring to the ascension of Acts 1.

- ॐ It was a literal act; there is no doubt about the Greek words in Acts 1:9. Four distinct words are used to describe ascension, and the Second Coming will come in "like manner."

- ॐ Christ arrived in heaven (Acts 2:33-36, 3:21, 7:55, 56; Romans 8:34; Ephesians 1:20-22; 4:8-10; Revelation 1:7, etc.).

Meaning of Ascension

❦ End of earthly ministry, time for Holy Spirit.

❦ Position of Christ in heaven is one of lordship; seated at right hand of God awaiting earth becoming His footstool and Davidic throne set up (Matthew 25:31).

V. FUTURE PLANS OR EXALTATION OF CHRIST

Christ's Present Work in Heaven

❦ High priest over true tabernacle on high (Hebrews 8:1, 2).

❦ Bestower of gifts (Romans 12:3-8; 1 Corinthians 12:4-11) to every believer who will enjoy the power of the gift only when life is wholly yielded to God (Romans 12:1, 2, 6-8; Philippians 2:13). Christ also bestows certain gifted men to local congregations (Ephesians 4:7-11; 1 Corinthians 12:11, 18).

❦ Intercession for believer (John 17:1-26) and care of believer (Peter; Luke 22:31, 32).

❦ Advocate for believer; appears before God on behalf of men (1 John 1:9, 2:1; Hebrews 9:24-28; Revelation 12:10).

Christ's Present Work on Earth

❦ He indwells the church (Matthew 28:18-20; John 14:18, 20; Colossians 1:27) to prepare it and us for His Second Coming; positional truth.

❦ Has sent Holy Spirit to accomplish present work of believers in this age (John 14:23); fellowship truth.

❦ Rapture—first phase of Second Coming; coming for His saints.

❦ Scripture references in John 14:2, 3; 1 Thessalonians 4:13-18; John 5:28, 29; 1 Corinthians 15:51-58. Not revealed in Old Testament (Romans 16:25, 26; Colossians 1:26).

❦ New bodies of believers of this age—sinless and glorified (Ephesians 5:27; Philippians 3:20, 21; 1 Corinthians 15:51).

- Second Coming with His saints—second phase of Second Coming.
- Contrasts between rapture and Second Coming, which are seven years apart (tribulation).
  - Rapture—earth to heaven—Father's house; Second Coming—heaven to earth.
  - Rapture—living saints translated; not so in Second Coming.
  - Rapture—saints to heaven; Second Coming—saints remain on earth.
  - Rapture—world unchanged; Second Coming—world judged and changed.
  - Rapture—deliverance from day of wrath that follows; Second Coming—deliverance from wrath that has been.
  - Rapture described as imminent; Second Coming preceded by signs, etc.
  - Rapture revealed only in New Testament; Second Coming in Old and New Testaments.
  - Rapture deals only with believers; Second Coming deals with both saved and unsaved.
  - Rapture relates to church; Second Coming to Israel and gentile believers and unbelievers.
  - Rapture unseen by world; Second Coming seen.

Events That Precede Second Coming

- After rapture, a confederacy will be formed out of which a strong dictator will emerge.
- A short period of peace and a covenant with Israel.
- A persecution of Israel and believers in Christ; great strife and problems on earth for 3½ years until Christ returns with His saints and hosts of heaven to straighten out the mess and rule for 1,000 years.
- His millennial reign on earth, to fulfill covenants given Israel and prove blessing of harmony with God.
- The kingdom age (Isaiah 11:1-16, 65:17, 66:22; 2 Peter 3:13;

Revelation 21:1), after millennial reign; comes according to Revelation 20, 21.

✦ Satan released from abyss.

✦ Armies formed to revolt against God; they are defeated.

✦ Passing of old heaven and earth.

✦ Great white-throne judgment.

✦ Creation of new heaven and earth.

✦ Descent of bridal city out of heaven.

✦ Christ reigns forever (2 Samuel 7:16; Psalms 89:20-37; Isaiah 9:6, 7; Luke 1:31; Revelation 11:15).

VI. Special Teachings Emphasized in the Person and Work of Christ

Historical Views of the Person of Christ

✦ Ebionites—denied Christ's divine nature but admitted that He received supernatural powers at baptism; still, held that Christ was not divine.

✦ Gnostics—some denied reality of Christ's human body; others said there was a nonmaterial body; others said Jesus and Christ were different.

✦ Arians—Christ first of created beings through whom all others and things were and are made.

✦ Appolinarians—denied integrity of human nature of Christ.

✦ Nestorians—denied union of divine and human natures of Christ.

✦ Euthchians—Christ's humanity different from ours; opposite of Nestorians, said Christ was only one divine nature.

✦ Our view (Biblical view)—Christ has two natures, human and divine, each complete and true; two natures are organically and indissolvably united, yet no third nature is formed. We do not divide Christ or confound the natures.

Two Natures of Christ

- He was human.
  - He was recognized; walked, talked, was weary, ate, drank, slept, etc., besides having a human parent and brother and sisters; grew (Luke 2:40, 52); suffered and died.
  - He was and is the perfect human, and never submitted to temptation (2 Corinthians 5:21).
- He was divine.
  - Divine names (John 20:28; 1 John 5:20; Romans 9:5); called "Son of God," "Lord."
  - Divine: equality (John 17:5, 12:45); relationship (John 10:30; 2 Corinthians 13:14); worship (Matthew 2:2, 11).
  - Divine attributes (Matthew 28:18; John 11:25, 26; Colossians 1:16, 17).

Names and Titles of Christ (Not Exhaustive)

- Jesus, Christ, Messiah, Lord, I Am, Son of God, Son of Man, Son of Abraham, Son of David, Son of the Highest, Second Man, Last Adam, The Word, Emmanuel, Savior, Rabbi, Master.
- HE IS EVERYTHING!

Pneumatology
Doctrine of the Holy Spirit

❧❧

INTRODUCTION

The word *pneumatology* is derived from the Greek word for spirit, which is *pneuma* (silent *p*). Until lately, there has been a strange neglect of the study of the Holy Spirit. There are even some theology books that do not devote a special section to study of the Holy Spirit (Strong's *Systematic Theology* (1907) and Thiessen (1949) are examples). We grant that the Holy Spirit is often referred to in relationship to other members of the Godhead and in redemptive roles, but no distinct study is put forth in many older works and studies.

Praise the Lord this is being rectified today, though probably as a reaction to many false teachings and errors that have arisen. The Pentecostal and charismatic errors of today have probably arisen because of the misuse of Biblical terms and a general misunderstanding of the doctrine of the Holy Spirit. Misunderstanding of signs such as the gifts of tongues and healing, and the great emphasis on terms such as "Baptism of the Holy Spirit," might have been avoided if believers had recognized that the Spirit is the unseen, quiet member of the Trinity whose ministry is to bring attention to Christ and the Father. The Spirit is not set forth as an object of faith, as are the Father (Romans 4:24) and the Son (John 3:16) for salvation. Rather, the Holy Spirit is the executive and executor of the Godhead—and a good executive doesn't draw attention to himself, but instead executes so effectively that another person or entire company receives the attention and success.

First, we will study this doctrine as a whole (the characteristics and work of the Holy Spirit in all ages), and then endeavor to deal with some of the modern-day questions and problems regarding the Holy Spirit.

I. THE HOLY SPIRIT IS A PERSON

The Holy Spirit is not an "it" without personality and personal identification. Though He does not speak of or refer to Himself, He is not neuter but masculine, and is an integral part of the Godhead with His own personality and task. *Special note:* Though the Greek noun for *Spirit* is neuter in most cases, the pronoun is masculine, thus emphasizing personality. Normally a neuter noun always calls for a neuter pronoun, but the change in this instance makes a case for emphasis. Read John 1:18 and chapters 7, 14, and 16.

- As a person, the Holy Spirit has characteristics, an identification, and a task; He does what a person does. Specifically,
  - He teaches (John 14:26, 16:13-15; 1 John 2:27).
  - He speaks (Galatians 4:6).
  - He leads (Acts 8:29, 10:19, 13:2, 16:6, 7, 20:23, 28; Romans 8:14; Galatians 5:18).
  - He intercedes (Romans 8:26).
  - He proves the world (John 16:8).
  - He regenerates (John 3:6).
  - He seals (Ephesians 4:30).
  - He baptizes (1 Corinthians 12:13).
  - He fills (Ephesians 5:18).

- As a person, He is involved with other persons. Men may:
  - vex Him by grieving Him (Ephesians 4:30).
  - quench (resist) Him (1 Thessalonians 5:19).
  - blaspheme Him (Matthew 12:3).
  - lie to Him (Acts 5:3).
  - disrespect Him (Hebrews 10:29).
  - speak against Him (Matthew 12:32).

- The Bible refers to the Holy Spirit as a person (e.g., John 14:16, 17, 26, 16:7; 1 John 2:1, 2).

- The Holy Spirit is co-equal with the Father and the Son, who are also personalities.

- The Holy Spirit is called God (Acts 5:3, 4; 2 Corinthians 3:18 [ASV]).

- He has the attributes of God (Genesis 1:2; John 26:13; 1 Corinthians 2:9-11).

- He does the work of God (Psalms 104:30; Luke 12:11, 12; Acts 1:5, 20:28; 1 Corinthians 6:11).

II. THE HOLY SPIRIT'S WORK IN THE VARIOUS AGES

During the present age, the Holy Spirit came very visibly at Pentecost to administer things of God on earth through the church. Does that mean the Holy Spirit wasn't working on the earth in previous dispensations? Of course not. In addition to being present everywhere as omnipresent God, He had specific duties and functions in all previous ages.

Function of the Holy Spirit in Old Testament Days

- He was, as in all ages, present everywhere.

- He worked in and through people from the beginning to the end of the Old Testament (Genesis 41:38 (Joseph); Exodus 31:3, 35:31; Numbers 27:18; Job 33:4; Psalms 139:7; Haggai 2:4, 5; Zechariah 4:6).

- Many specific functions of the Holy Spirit in the Old Testament:
  - Creation—"let us" in Genesis.
  - Inspiration (2 Peter 1:21).
  - Came upon men for special power (Exodus 35:31 [Saul, David, etc.]); John 17:14 teaches that the Spirit "shall be in you" later on in dispensation of grace, so Spirit was *with* Old Testament saints but did not indwell them (Judges 3:10, 11:29, 14:6).

Holy Spirit during Days of Christ

- Holy Spirit conceived Christ in Mary's womb, came upon Christ as a dove at baptism, and indwelt Christ (Hebrews 9:41) in a unique way; left Christ temporarily while He was on the cross ("My God ... why hast Thou forsaken?").

- Men during that time could ask for Spirit (Luke 11:13), though Scripture doesn't tell us of any who did ask. According to John 20:22, Christ gave the Spirit for temporary strength and wisdom until Pentecost when the Spirit would permanently abide in believers' hearts (John 14:16).

Holy Spirit during Church Age

- He was promised by the Father (John 14:16, 17) and Christ (John 16:7), and came into the world in a unique relationship at Pentecost now to abide in world.

- Ministry to lost in world (John 16:7-11).

- Conviction of the sin of unbelief in Christ. Not *sins*: this just increases guilt, but rather *sin*, the lost condition of man and need for a Savior, the new sin that could not have been committed until after Christ died and was resurrected. Christ bore our penalty for all other sins. The Spirit convicts the sinner of the one sin of unbelief.

- Holy Spirit convicts the unsaved (John 6:44; Romans 8:28-30).

- Righteousness—the righteousness of God and the inadequacy of man's righteousness to satisfy God; the blessed truth of imputed righteousness given to believers as the gift of God, whereby the believer becomes as righteous as God by accepting Christ (Romans 5:17; Ephesians 1:6).

- Judgment—God's judgment of sin, hatred of sin, and the fact that Christ was judged for sin.

- Ministry to world as a restrainer—so that Satan and sin will not overwhelm world and believers (2 Thessalonians 2:3-10).

The human heart and world are desperately wicked and will run rampant when the "restrainer" is removed (Jeremiah 17:9; Ephesians 2:2, 3).

❧ Ministry to believers in many areas, such as regeneration, guidance, sealing, indwelling, baptizing, filling, etc. (see later in this section).

God the Spirit ministers to the immaterial part of man. Today this is termed psychology by some, but to the Christian the great psychology book is the Bible, which does affirm in numerous places (such as Romans 8:5-27, especially v. 16) that God is in custody of the believer's inner self.

III. SCRIPTURAL SYMBOLS AND TYPES OF THE HOLY SPIRIT

There are seven basic classifications of figures of speech, all found in the Bible and used by the Holy Spirit to teach truth. They are metaphors, similes, symbols, types, parables, allegories, and emblems.

❧ Metaphor: "I am bread"

❧ Simile: "I am vine" (stronger and longer-lasting than metaphor)

❧ Symbol: fire, dove, water

❧ Type: Ark, a type of salvation

❧ Parable: e.g., Matthew 13:18 (KJV)—"Hear ye therefore the parable of the sower"

❧ Allegory: Pilgrim's Progress

❧ Emblem: lion of tribe of Judah

Likewise, the Holy Spirit Himself is presented under various types and symbols:

❧ Oil: Meal offering (Leviticus 2:1-16) or anointing oil; altar, Christ's death (Exodus 40:10, 13, 15); Aaron—Spirit on

Christ, sons of Aaron—believers of this age (Exodus 30:22-32); oil of gladness (Exodus 30) and oil used for:

- Healing
- Comfort
- Illumination
- Anointing/consecration

- Water: The most plentiful substance on earth. It is used for:
  - Cleansing—It is vital to the child of God for its threefold work:
    - Spirit applies blood of Christ for cleansing.
    - Spirit dwells within.
    - Spirit's manifestations flow out.
  - Scriptural references include laver (John 3, 4; Genesis 1; etc.).
  - Satisfying.
  - Reviling—Pharaoh.
  - Refreshing.

- Fire: Used as a symbol of several things in Scripture, of which the Spirit is one. It is used to signify the Holy Spirit in:
  - Seven lamps of fire—light (Revelation 4:5).
  - Cloven tongues—power (Acts 2:3).
  - Zeal and fervor of service—sacrifice.

- Wind (Isaiah 40:24; John 3:8).

- Dove (John 1:30-34 [Noah]).

- Earnest (a sort of down payment) on our eternal hope: gifts to Rebecca, fruit of Canaan, gifts of Boaz (2 Corinthians 1:22).

- Seal: ownership by God, authority, genuineness, and unchangeableness; completed transaction; value (Ephesians 1:13, 14).

- Abraham's servant (Genesis 24).

IV. THE HOLY SPIRIT IN RELATION TO THE CHRISTIAN

The majority of Scriptural references to the Holy Spirit occur in relation to this subject. The Spirit has seven ministries in the world: (1) restrainer in world; (2) convicter of the unsaved; (3) regeneration; (4) indwelling; (5) sealing; (6) baptism; (7) filling. The first two of these have already been covered; we now go on to the latter five, which relate to the believer.

Regeneration

ॐ Defined—new life, new birth, spiritual resurrection, the new creation (Titus 3:5). It is the new supernatural life that believers receive as sons (children) of God.

ॐ Though all three persons of the Trinity are involved in the regeneration of the believer, the Holy Spirit is specifically the regenerator (John 3:3-7; Titus 3:5).

ॐ Results of regeneration:
- ॐ Eternal life is imparted: born again eternally (John 3); alive from dead (Romans 6:13); new creation (2 Corinthians 5:17).
- ॐ A new nature is given (Ephesians 4:24).
- ॐ The new life is given capacity for new experiences—new life, relationships, eyes, ears, etc., are complemented by the indwelling Spirit (1 Corinthians 2:9, 10).
- ॐ Eternal security—we cannot unregenerate ourselves.

Indwelling (Sometimes Called Anointing)

ॐ Defined (John 14:17)—The Holy Spirit literally lives in the body of the believer (Romans 8:9; Jude 19; John 7:37-39; Romans 5:5).

ॐ It is universal (all believers receive Spirit).

ॐ It occurs at the moment of salvation (new life, new man, etc.).

ॐ Some questions arise in some people's minds because of delayed indwellings recorded in Acts 8:14-17 and 19:1-6. This was because of transitional time—Old Testament passages and Luke 11:13. All explained by dispensational teaching.

⁓ Indwelling is a characterizing feature of this age (John 14:17; Romans 7:6, 8:9; 1 Corinthians 6:19, 20).

Sealing

The Holy Spirit validates, identifies with, secures, and completes our salvation by becoming our seal at the moment of salvation (Ephesians 1:13; 2 Corinthians 1:21).

Baptism

Probably the most confusion in pneumatology concerns this teaching (Acts 1:5; Romans 6:1-4; 1 Corinthians 12:13; Ephesians 4:5). Some confusion lies in the fact that in some instances filling and baptism both happened at same time; nevertheless, these are distinct occurrences, as are indwelling, sealing, etc.

⁓ Defined as being placed into the body of Christ.

⁓ All mentions (there are eleven in all) before Pentecost refer to a future event that had not happened previously (Matthew 3:11; Mark 1:8; Luke 3:16; John 1:33; Acts 1:5).

⁓ Two things happen at baptism. The believer is:
  ⁃ Placed into the body of Christ (Acts 2:47; 1 Corinthians 6:15, 12:12-14).
  ⁃ Placed into Christ (John 14:20; Colossians 2:12); identification with Christ.

⁓ An error to watch for is making baptism of Spirit into a "spiritual experience" subsequent to salvation and thinking that an evidence of this is speaking in tongues. Though this did happen in a few instances in Acts, it is not consistent, and Acts is a transitional book. Tongues are not even mentioned in filling of Spirit, or in conversion of Cornelius in Acts 10; 11. Acts 11:15-17 is just the Lord's confirmation that gentiles can receive the Lord as Jews did before in this dispensation.

Filling

A most important teaching in relation to salvation, but one of the most confused teachings in many Christians' minds. Filling is part of the Christian experience regarding power and service, and is a repeated experience in a believer's life—in contrast to salvation and Spirit sealing, indwelling, regenerating, and baptizing, which are singular, once-and-for-all experiences.

Filling is very important to the believer. To be filled is to be a happy, fulfilled Christian; not to be filled is to be a carnal, unhappy believer who is feeling guilty and striving to find happiness in the world, or has given up, resigning himself to a life of drudgery and frustration just waiting for death or the Rapture. God is faithful to give us all that we need for salvation from the power of sin today, and the power over sin today is the indwelling Holy Spirit. To be filled with the Spirit is to be submissive to the Spirit, to be under His control—better to *want* to be under His control and to seek His will in one's life *today*.

If I am filled today, it is because I've become conscious of the Lord, spoken to Him in prayer, realized that I can invest today in eternity, and knowingly sought His will, leading, and influence in my life. My decisions will reflect the Spirit's leading and now I know that today is the Lord's. I will pick up my cross carefully and go on my way.

Filling of the Holy Spirit before Pentecost

- ☙ Certain individuals had the Spirit come upon them before Pentecost (e.g., Exodus 28:3 [Bezelel], 31:3, 35:31) to accomplish certain tasks. It was usually temporary or until the task was done, as illustrated in the time of the Judges (Judges 3:10, 11:29, 14:6, 19) or Saul (1 Samuel 11:6, in contrast to 16:14 and 18:10).

- ☙ There was no indication that filling happened as a result of yielding; rather, it occurred on the basis of God's sovereign need to accomplish something through a man. Thus, many kings, judges, prophets, etc., were empowered.

Filling of the Holy Spirit after Pentecost

- After Pentecost came a new age, when Spirit would work through every believer; each believer is now a royal priest (1 Peter 2:5). Illustrations of the Spirit's working are found in Acts 2:4, 4:8, 4:31, 6:3, 6:5; 7:55, etc.; also Ephesians 5:18.

- Filling of the believer is accomplished only under special conditions (described later). A believer is either filled or not—it is not a matter of partial filling or maturity. A believer is commanded to be filled in Ephesians 5:18 and to be otherwise is disobedience.

- Definition of filling—"The spiritual state where the Holy Spirit is fulfilling all that He came to do in the heart and life of the individual believer. . . . Every believer is saved to glorify God as a member of Christ's body on earth, we are saved to function, every believer will under the Spirit do exactly as God would have him do and rejoice in that ministry" (Chafer, 1947–1948, vol. VI).

  When one is in this state he is filled. When the believer interjects, through his sinful nature, his own plans, desires, and lusts, he loses the filling and is carnal. He remains carnal until he confesses that sin and acknowledges that all work done for the Lord in a carnal state is wasted, for it is thus works of the flesh: "wood, hay and stubble." Only work of the Lord accomplished through the leading of the Spirit is valid for the reward of "gold, silver, and precious stone." The judgment seat involves discerning God's work done by the Spirit through a man, as opposed to work accomplished through the energy of the flesh. A person may be filled many times, as illustrated in use of the Greek present tense in Ephesians 5:18.

- God works through a filled Christian without hindrance.

- Maturity and filling are not the same, though there's an obvious relationship between them. Maturity comes through growth in the Word and spiritual experiences as a result of filling; discernment as to spiritual things is the result. Obviously, time is a factor, although some mature faster than others because of their love of the Lord and time spent in the Word with a tender heart. A spirit-filled Christian matures more rapidly.

➤ Filling can be enjoyed by a babe in Christ as well as mature believers—maturity comes faster the longer we are under the control of (filled by) the Spirit.

➤ Many passages speak of growth (Ephesians 4:11-16; 1 Peter 2:2; 2 Peter 3:18; Matthew 13:30). These passages refer to maturity.

➤ Conditions for filling by the Holy Spirit.

  ➤ First, important—a negative! Filling is *not* accomplished through praying—and it is not a special second experience that comes after salvation and renders the believer holy and more acceptable to God.

     To add to Scripture is the sin of Satan and Eve in the beginning chapters of Genesis—and though to some it seems reasonable to pray for filling, doing so is not Scriptural. There is only one instance in Scripture where Christ mentions praying for reception of the Spirit (Luke 11:13). That was before Pentecost and during Christ's lifetime. To the Jews, that was a tremendous opportunity to accept God's plan for the Jewish age to be fulfilled, by accepting Christ as the Messiah and thereby receive the Holy Spirit for power to tell this message of Christ being Messiah to a darkened age.

     After Pentecost, in our present age of grace and the church, the Holy Spirit automatically indwells the believer. This is in accordance with the promise found in Luke 24:49; John 7:38, 39, 14:16, 17; and Acts 1:4, 5. It is later confirmed as an historic fact in Romans 8, 9, and 15; 1 Corinthians 6:19; 2 Corinthians 1:22; Galatians 4:6; and 1 John 2:20, 27. (See also Acts 2:4.) For the Christian, to go back to Luke 11:13 is to ignore subsequent truth.

  ➤ Prayer for Spirit's filling is error. The Spirit does not withhold blessing until prevailed upon, nor is He reluctant to bless the believer until something on God's part is broken down.

- The Holy Spirit is anxious to work in the believer and will do so immediately upon the believer's making way for the Spirit to work. The Spirit fills or controls instantly when the Christian clears the way for the Spirit to work; this clearing of self is described later. Prayer and waiting for filling are not a condition of Spirit-filling. The disciples waited 10 days at Pentecost, not for their own filling but for the advent of the Spirit into the world.
- The Holy Spirit's filling is not dependent upon a crisis experience of supreme effort. It was made possible at Pentecost for the advent of the Spirit into the world.

- Recognize that the Holy Spirit indwells you and wants to accomplish a spiritual work through you (Ephesians 2:10; Acts 4:8, 31, 9:17; Acts 13:9 [Paul]).

- Recognize that the Holy Spirit not only indwells you but also wants to fill you; even as wine controls the body and functions of an inebriated individual, so the Spirit wishes to control all of our functions (Ephesians 5:18).

- "Quench not the Spirit" (1 Thessalonians 5:19). He wants to fill us, so don't stop Him! *Quenching* is like stifling or dousing a fire, refusing to let a fire get started, or taking fuel away. To the Christian, it is no fuel (time in the Word) or no oxygen (thinking about and seeking spiritual things). Quenching means stifling or suppressing the Spirit as He speaks to us. It is being unwilling to let the Spirit have His way. Satan rebelled (Isaiah 14:14), whereas Christ submitted (Luke 22:42). Thus, we are to submit to the Spirit. How do I submit to or fuel the Spirit rather than quench Him?
  - Surrender one's life to the Lord (Romans 6:13, 12:1, 2). We serve either God or Satan (Matthew 6:24). God the Spirit awaits you to present yourself to Him and acknowledge Him as your master; since salvation, this is reasonable. It is not a matter of "giving to God" a particular issue, but rather deciding to take God's will for one's life; making God's will final. "Quench not the Spirit" is in the present tense, indicating that it is a continuous experience begun by an initial act of surrender.

- Yieldedness to the Word of God, its exhortations, and its truth; to refuse is to "quench."
- Yieldedness to the Holy Spirit's guidance; to refuse is to "quench."
- Yieldedness to unpleasant situations of life; to grumble, complain, etc., is to "quench." Look at Israel's wanderings. Suffering for Christ is Scriptural (Philippians 1:29) and the supreme example is Christ (Philippians 2:5-11).

- "Grieve not the Spirit" (Ephesians 4:30). This deals with sin in the life of the believer.
  - When sin is not dealt with, the Spirit is grieved and guidance, instruction, fellowship, and power are hindered. Restoration comes only through confession.
  - Continual grieving of the Spirit results in chastisement (Hebrews 12:5-15; 1 Corinthians 11:31, 32).

- "Walk by the Spirit" (Galatians 5:16). This is a command to appropriate exercise of the power and blessing provided by the indwelling Spirit. It is to anticipate and expect the Spirit to work through you. It is to recognize that we were saved to accomplish something for God.
  - It is an act of faith—expecting great things that only God can do through us, as described in 2 Corinthians 10:5 and John 13:34, 15:12.
  - It is to bear fruit (Galatians 5:22, 23).
  - It is to pray in power (1 Thessalonians 5:16-18).
  - It is to defeat Satan (Ephesians 6:10-20).

Results of Holy Spirit Filling an Individual

The following points are drawn from Chafer (1947–1948):

- Progressive sanctification—fruit of spirit is manifested in my life (Galatians 5:22, 23).
- Spirit will illuminate spiritual truth (John 16:12-14).
- Spirit will guide (Romans 12:2); "perfect will of God" (Genesis 24:27; Romans 8:14; Galatians 5:18).

- ❧ Assurance of salvation (Romans 8:16; Galatians 4:6; 1 John 3:24, 4:13).
- ❧ True worship and love of God now possible (Ephesians 5:18-21).
- ❧ True prayer fellowship now possible (Romans 8:26).
- ❧ Believer's service and exercise of spiritual gifts now valid (John 7:38, 39).

V. THE DOCTRINE OF SPIRITUAL GIFTS

This matter is addressed in Romans 12:3-8; 1 Corinthians 12:27, 28; and Ephesians 4:7-16. The Lord wants us to know about spiritual gifts (1 Corinthians 12:1). The problem today does not seem to lie in lack of knowledge that spiritual gifts exist, but rather in discovering our gifts and utilizing them to the glory of God.

- ❧ Definition of spiritual gifts: "A gift is a Divine enablement wrought in and through the believer by the Spirit who indwells him" (Chafer, vol. 6, 1948). The Spirit works within a believer to accomplish certain divine purposes through that believer; the tools given to that believer to accomplish that job are the spiritual gifts.
- ❧ There are also "gifts to the church," as described in Ephesians 4:7-11. These are people gifted by God to build up ("edify") the church (Ephesians 4:12-16). They are: (1) apostles (past), (2) prophets (past), (3) evangelists, and (4) pastor-teachers.

Listing of Spiritual Gifts

The possible variety of gifts is innumerable, because no two lives are lived under the same conditions. Some of the gifts listed in Scripture are temporary: "sign" gifts bestowed until the canon was completed so that the message given by God's men could be authenticated in apostolic days. Other gifts are listed, but obviously an exhaustive list of gifts, either to the believer or to the church, is not possible. Following are some spiritual gifts (1 Corinthians 12:4-11).

⁕ Word of wisdom (permanent gift)—Gifts of understanding and discernment; counseling gift; ability to understand and relate doctrine to all situations of life (James 1:5). Now bestowed by grace.

⁕ Word of knowledge—Ability to understand and categorize the Word and teach it.

Temporary Gifts

Temporary, sign gifts of that day and others included helps, governments (administration), and tongues. For temporary gifts, the key word is "faith" in 1 Corinthians 12:9; this changed after canon was complete, as described in Romans 10:17. An order of importance is given in 1 Corinthians 12:28-30—note the word "first." See also the discussion of tongues in section VI of this chapter.

⁕ Faith (1 Corinthians 12:9).

⁕ Healing (1 Corinthians 12:9).

⁕ Working of miracle (1 Corinthians 12:10).

⁕ Prophecy (1 Corinthians 12:10).

⁕ Discerning of spirits (1 Corinthians 12:10).

⁕ Tongues (1 Corinthians 12:10).

⁕ Interpretation of tongues (1 Corinthians 12:10).

We believe we must study Scripture and rightly divide it (2 Timothy 2: 14-18). Some will subvert the Word to the hurt of the hearers. Part of rightly dividing is to recognize that although certain portions of Scripture contain specific instructions for certain people in certain ages, all Scripture contains principles of God's working with people and thus is profitable. Greatest truth of Scripture is that *God communicates with people: We are not to be left in the dark*, and as Scripture unfolds greater communication is possible.

⁕ *Rightly dividing.* We do not follow Nazarite vows today, nor Jewish dietary regulations, even as we do not slay lambs and set up altars—but these rules and actions were right in their time and place. Likewise, we don't have tongues and healings by individuals to prove God's power upon an individual today, because we have the Word, which abundantly proves God's power by recording the past works of God in creation, Moses, Elijah, Christ, and the apostles. This need not be proven again: We have the Word, and we know that God will work in power and will heal (but not through individual "healers") and work miracles as needed to accomplish His work. We are all God's priests and all of us in the body should be telling the message. Our power comes from the filling of the Spirit and allowing Him to work through us to glorify Christ rather than individuals.

ﾟ *Faith is the better way.* Today God points out, as illustrated by Thomas in John 20, that we are to walk by faith, believing things unseen (Hebrews 11:1). We are not to demand spectacular signs of tongues and healing and great movements, but rather are to believe the Word and its promises and lean daily on the Lord. If He chooses to do something visible and spectacular through us, that's all right, but we do not live dependent on great signs and evidences of God's working. We are just to live by faith and watch God's program unfold. In these last days before Christ's return, there will be great darkness and sin, but He will remain faithful. The important matter today is not healing, but the fact that "my grace is sufficient for you" (2 Corinthians 12:9). God will provide inner happiness, peace, and stability for every situation. Do you believe it?

ﾟ *Healing today.* First, true healing today is by God's sovereign decision; it can be miraculous and as a result of prayer, but is not accomplished through agents (healers). Second, healing today can be done by God working through a physician or other health care professional, for all health and every "good gift" is from God.

  ↝ So-called divine healers today often seem to be effective, although upon investigation many healers turn out to be less effective than they claim—or outright frauds.

- One explanation is a temporary, psychological type of "mind over matter" recovery or healing that later disappears. Another is the removal of an indwelling demon that can possess an unbeliever and cause loss of health.
- If God chooses not to heal, as He did Paul in 2 Corinthians 12:9, then we look to God for His grace to endure. We trust Him and live victoriously to the glory of God.

Gifts to Church

Gifts to the church (described earlier and in Ephesians 4:7-19):

- Apostles—to start church.
- Prophets—before canon done.
- Teachers—today.

Ministry Gifts

There are also ministering gifts (Romans 12:3-8):

- Prophecy (Romans 12:6).
- Ministry—helping others (Romans 12:7).
- Teaching (Romans 12:7).
- Exhorting (Romans 12:8).
- Giving (Romans 12:8).
- Ruling (Romans 12:8).
- Mercy (Romans 12:8).

Spiritual Gifts Confirmed by Experience

Why study spiritual gifts?

- Harmony with local church and the church invisible and universal.
- Understanding of all believers and congregations not to be same; ministries vary.

- Criticism stops; one person is gifted for one ministry, another person for another.

- Tension, judging, lack of harmony stop; "shoe-horning" of people into jobs stops. Illustrations are Paul as an apostle/teacher; Barnabas as a counselor/helper.

- Harmony within one's self. Not all believers are the same or called to do same work in same way; only immaturity demands that it must be done "my way." All are to witness, but not all are evangelists. All are to have love (fruit of the Spirit), but not all are effective in hospital callings and nursing home ministries (gift of mercy). All are to be faithful in work, but not all can administer (gift of government). Not all are good at "helps" (some are all thumbs), but they can give other assistance. We learn our gift(s) and are not jealous, frustrated, or guilty when we realize we don't have the same gift as another.

- Understanding of this truth not only helps us to understand that all do not serve identically, but also helps us to become more efficient and effective, as assignments are made in harmony with gifts.

- Eliminate pride. Some feel that their gift is result of their goodness or effort. *It is not*; it is God-given. Also, should eliminate false modesty (1 Corinthians 12:24).

- Helps ease family and marital problems; spouses stop badgering mates into some kind of spiritual mold and understand when other spouse is busy in ministry.

Teachings on Spiritual Gifts

- We are to know about spiritual gifts (1 Corinthians 12:1).

- Spiritual gifts are imparted to us at the moment of salvation by a sovereign act of the Spirit (Romans 12:6; 1 Corinthians 12:8-11, 18). These are described in the aorist tense in Greek, which connotes completion in some time past and the position of the believer.

❧ All believers receive one or more gifts (Ephesians 2:10); this is theme of whole chapter of 1 Corinthians 12; also Ephesians 4:7.

❧ There is a diversity of gifts (Romans 12:6; 1 Corinthians 12:4-11; Ephesians 4:11), but all believers are to have fruit of the Spirit (Galatians 5) and perform as priests (Hebrews 13:15, 16).

❧ The blessing and power of the gift will be experienced only by those who are wholly yielded to God (Romans 12:1, 2, 6-8). Spirit-filled believers are constantly active in the exercise of their gifts. Carnal believers do not actively exercise their gifts and often don't know them; however, by confession of sin, yieldedness, and study of the Word, they learn of them and use them.

❧ The giving of gifts assures that each believer has his or her particular place and function and opportunity to serve God in the framework of his or her own personality and gifts (1 Corinthians 12:12-31; Ephesians 4:16). Thus, as each member of the body differs, it makes sense for the whole body to be well planned and organized. 1 Corinthians 12:7 says that gifts are profitable, so implication is that service done in energy of flesh is unprofitable (Ephesians 2:10).

❧ The term *spiritual gifts* is to be understood as completely different from the common meaning given to the word *gift* today: the latter sense refers to a native ability or talent received at birth, such as artistic ability, musical facility, teaching ability, etc. The spiritual gift is a ministry of the indwelling Holy Spirit performing through a believer as an instrument. A good schoolteacher may be a poor Bible teacher because he does not have the spiritual gift—the spiritual gift does not refer to a natural talent or a place.

❧ Spiritual gifts are not secured by seeking, but are sovereignly given by the Holy Spirit at salvation time (1 Corinthians 12:11). In the apostolic church, some gifts were given to continue throughout the church age, and some sign gifts apparently stopped after the first generation of Christians. Every gift is subject to regulation by the Word of God; thus, they shouldn't be a basis for pride, but rather somber acceptance, for every believer will have to give an account of his or her acceptance and exercise of gifts. Many misinterpret 1 Corinthians 12:31 and 14:1 because they don't know these verses are written in the second person (plural "ye"), describing the church desiring and praying for certain people with these gifts. Why? To edify the church. This explains why those who are continually telling people to ask God for the gift of tongues, etc., are misguided.

≫ Gift is a special capacity for development by rebirth.

How to Find One's Gift(s)

Even believers sometimes wonder: What is my gift? Here are some suggestions for discovering your gift(s):

≫ In some cases, like love, when you have it, you know it.

≫ Pulpit instruction and teaching.

≫ Counseling with Spirit-filled, mature believers.

≫ Objective self-searching. Look honestly at your life and efforts. Are you never asked to chair a committee, or have you left jobs unfinished or half-done, even when your heart was right? (no government gift). Do you have hard responses to pleas for help? (no mercy gift). Be careful not to delude yourself into thinking that you have a glamorous gift by your own desires and aspirations, and not to act in certain ways because others expect it of you—that is hypocrisy.

≫ Answer these questions as you seek your gift:
  ↦ What is my greatest concern for my church?
  ↦ What is lacking in the life of my church? What do I notice? How can I help?
  ↦ Have spiritually mature people told me of certain abilities I possess? Paul saw some things in Timothy that Timothy evidently knew nothing about.

- What am I often asked to do?
- Do others often express appreciation for one ministry over another?
- While in perfect fellowship with the Lord, do certain gifts hold no appeal for me, whereas others do?
- Have I honestly prayed, seeking the Lord's guidance in this area of my life?

- Now begin to minister; don't wait for all the answers. Volunteer—step out in faith!

- Recognize that to develop gifts is work (Ephesians 2:10). Gifts are not ornaments—they are given for service: "Whatsoever thy hand findeth to do, do it with thy might" (Ecclesiastes 9:10).

VI. THE HOLY SPIRIT AND TONGUES

The subject of gifts today has two controversial areas: namely, tongues and healing. Healing was discussed in section V of this chapter, but we should investigate tongues in greater depth because of the present-day strife it has caused. We will study each instance in Scripture where the subject arises and then summarize our conclusions.

Before we begin the study, we must recognize that one of the minor controversies in this area is the question of whether the tongues referred to in Scripture are known languages or unknown "gibberish." Well-known, respected scholars have come down on both sides of the question, and the issue is not entirely clear. Though we take time to deal with this subject now, we feel that the issue in 1 Corinthians 12–14 and the instances in Acts is not whether tongues were understandable, but rather whether they were building (edifying) the body of Christ.

There is no doubt that, in Acts 2 at Pentecost, the tongues were languages foreign to the speakers but understood by the hearers: The miracle was in the speaking, not the hearing (Acts 2:4, 8-12). The tongues of Acts 2 were duplicated in Acts 10 and 19, and were recognized as the same phenomenon (known tongues). Note Acts 11:15 and 19:6, in which tongues and prophecy are united.

Every time the word "unknown" is used in 1 Corinthians 12–14 (KJV), it is italicized, indicating that it was added by the translators; it was not in the original manuscript. Strauss, Richard DeHaan, and a host of others feel that the tongues of 1 Corinthians 12–14 were known tongues; some feel they were not. I feel, too, that they were known tongues, for the following reasons:

- Prophecy in Isaiah 28:11, 12 talks of tongues of strange nations (context), and the sign to Jews was hearing message from gentile lips.

- In every passage in Scripture, the word used, *glossolalia*, refers to known tongues. Why change?

- Greek word *glossa* (meaning "language" or "tongue") combined with *lalia* ("speech," taken from *lalew*) always means speaking for communication, never incomprehensible babbling.

- According to 1 Corinthians 14:22, tongues are given as a sign to the unbelieving Jew to communicate the Gospel. How can there be communication if the sounds used are gibberish?

Paul evidently had the gift of speaking in many languages. Because of his travels, he had to know Greek, Hebrew, Cretan, Armenian, and Assyrian, as well as (possibly) many of the dialects mentioned in Acts 2. This would conform with 1 Corinthians 14:18: "I speak with tongues more than ye all." Paul never needed an interpreter in foreign lands as far as we know, but he never boasted of this language gift or flaunted it—in fact, he never even mentioned it. I feel it was the gift of tongues.

We'll carefully study each passage in which tongues are mentioned. With Scripture as the basis, we then identify mistakes that present-day "charismatics" make and problems that arise in their teachings. Finally, we summarize all of our beliefs and teachings about tongues.

Tongues Mentioned in Scripture

1 Corinthians 12–14

❦ Background of the city. Corinth was the greatest pleasure city of the Roman empire, with a population in excess of 500,000. Located on an isthmus between the Adriatic and Aegean Seas, it was a place where boats were hauled on rollers, over land, for a few thousand feet, thereby saving days of sailing and expense. The result was always a heavy transitory population of some of the roughest sailors, soldiers, merchants, etc. Corinth was rich, a famous sports center with the greatest sports games of the ancient world at that time. It was also famous for its loose living and the love cult of Aphrodite (Venus; the goddess of love), and lent itself to lax morals and spectacular habits.

❦ Background of church. Undoubtedly Paul wrote this epistle (1 Corinthians) because of the carnality of the believers in that church. They had not grown in knowledge of doctrine and were confused in areas of marriage, morals, the Lord's Supper, food given to idols, and even incest. In addition, they were confusing the primitive and idolatrous religious rituals of tongues with the Scriptural sign of tongues and spiritual sign gifts. Consequently, Paul wrote the letter of 1 Corinthians to that church.

OUTLINE OF 1 CORINTHIANS 12–14:

❦ Purpose of spiritual gifts (chapter 12).
  - Holy Spirit will lead, Satan confuse (12:2, 3).
  - Diversities within the church lead to unity and dependence upon one another rather than schism (12:4-11).
  - Diversity in gifts (12:4).
  - Diversity in ministry of gifts (12:5).
  - Diversity in procedures (12:6).
  - Diversity in distribution of gifts (12:7-10).
  - Diversity brings unity in Spirit (12:11).

- Analogy of the body (12:12-26).
- Application of analogy (12:27-30).

- Spiritual gifts regulated by love (12:31–13:13).
  - I show you a better way than just to display gifts.
  - Gifts of spirit must be preceded by fruit of Spirit, which must be preceded by filling of the Spirit (chapter 13).
  - Gifts good only if administered in love (13:1, 2).
  - Giving is good only if given in love (13:3).
  - Love described (13:4-7).
  - Love is better than our present incomplete knowledge (13:8-12).
  - Love is the greatest (13:13).

- Church is to be edified (chapter 14). Edification is to be through prophecy, not selfish ministry of tongues (14:1-20).

- Tongues are a sign for Israel and the unsaved (14:21-23).

- Regulations regarding ministry of gifts in a local church (14:23-35).

- Conclusion (14:36-40).

HIGHLIGHTS OF 1 CORINTHIANS 12–14:

- God wants us to know about spiritual gifts (12:1).

- Christians are now led by the Spirit; before salvation they were led by Satan (12:2, 3).

- There is diversity (differences between individuals in the Spirit's leading) within the church (12:4-11, 28-30).

- Every believer can be led by the Spirit (12:7).

- Every believer is gifted by the Spirit according to the Spirit's sovereign wisdom (12:8-11).

- All Christians were placed into the body of Christ (baptized by Spirit) (12:13-18).

- The purpose of being placed into body is to avoid schism and to have care for one another (12:25).

- Not all have same gifts (12:28-30), nor should we expect or want the same gifts.

After all this careful teaching on unity, Paul rebuked the Corinthians in 12:31, saying "but you covet earnestly the best gifts." In the Greek, the word for *covet earnestly* can be in second person indicative or imperative. The most common and correct use and interpretation would be in the indicative (plain statement of fact), but most misread it as an imperative. This is very important, because to translate this in the imperative is to teach completely the opposite of its context. Nevertheless, many—if not most—do this, not recognizing that to seek a gift is to take sovereignty away from God and cause the giving of gifts to be done on the basis of our choice after salvation. This is not Scriptural.

Paul says in 1 Corinthians 12:31 and chapter 13 that he wants to show the Corinthians a more excellent way to edify the body, or care for one another. He stresses that spiritual gifts are useless unless regulated by the fruit of love (chapter 13). In other words, gifts of the Spirit must be preceded by the fruit of the Spirit; that is, they must be preceded by control (filling) by the Spirit. The danger of fruitlessness is illustrated by five wasted gifts (13:1-3):

- Tongues (13:1).
- Prophecy, although this provided predictive and authoritative doctrine before canon was complete (13:2).
- Knowledge (13:2).
- Faith (13:2).
- Giving (13:3).

The definition of *love* appears in 13:4-7. Love is patient, kind, without jealousy; is not proud; is careful in its behavior; is not seeking for self; is not easily provoked; thinketh no evil; is trusting, optimistic, and enduring. To have such characteristics is to be filled with the Spirit and will settle all problems regarding spiritual gifts, including the vaunted charismatic tongues. Love never faileth (13:8; Ephesians 3:17-19), though gifts and the needs therefor will pass away.

Many believe that the gifts referred to in 13:8 were temporary gifts given until the canon was complete, as described in 13:10. For example, prophecy, in this context, is the predictive and authoritative preaching that was given to some until the New Testament was completed in AD 100; then the Bible became the final and perfect authority. Tongues ceased with the destruction of Jerusalem and the dispersion of the Jews, for tongues were a sign gift to the Jews (14:22) and not needed thereafter. The knowledge was the special doctrinal discernment given to some leaders in the pre-canon days to distinguish true leaders from false teachers. This, too, was not needed after the New Testament was completed. This is described in 13:10, where it says "that which is in part [v. 9 knowledge and prophecy] shall be done away." Following that are two illustrations of partial knowledge being replaced by a new maturity or development:

- Child.
- Mirror—face to face with Christ.

A summary of chapter 13 appears in 14:1. Follow love and desire "spirituals" within church.

- The greatest gift is of communicating the Word; least gift is tongues (14:2-26).
- Self-edification spoken of in verse 4 is childish and selfish; seek rather to edify the church (14:12, 17, 26). See also the rebuke of 14:14.
- What about tongues in private?
  - Personal edification minimized (14:14).
  - One small statement in verse 4, contrasted with many concerning whole church being edified.
  - Tongues in private okay, but we do not know how it edifies.
  - If tongues necessary in private for growth, why should they ever cease (14:8)?
  - Since tongues are a sign, how can private tongues be a sign?
  - Such people cause division.
- Tongue speaking is childish (v. 20) if it is not used correctly, mainly as a sign to the Jews (14:21, 22).
- Prophecy written to the Jews when their hearts were hardened. God said that a sign shall be when you hear the

message in another tongue; take it as a sign that dispersion is here (sixth cycle of chastisement) (Isaiah 28:11, 12).

⁜ The Jews were always demanding signs (note Matthew 12:28-39; John 4:48; 1 Corinthians 2). They should be wary as in Moses' day (Matthew 24:24; 2 Thessalonians 2:9).

⁜ Gentile believers rejected tongues as a sign (14:23).

⁜ Paul says in 14:39 to "forbid not to speak with tongues," because Jews were still in Jerusalem, but after AD 70 need for tongues would cease (13:8).

⁜ Regulations regarding tongues in the Corinthians' church (14:26-39).

⁜ All things to be done for edifying (14:26).

⁜ Number—2 or 3 (14:27).

⁜ No interpreter—no tongues (14:28).

⁜ Order one at a time—God not author of confusion (14:28-33a, 40).

⁜ Women silent in church, so far as tongues and prophecy (14:34, 35; 1 Timothy 2:11, 12). There are to be no women preachers, elders, or leaders over men. There were occasions when women prayed and even prophesied in church (note 1 Corinthians 11:5), but this was only when invited to do so by men (note 1 Corinthians 11 context). Women were never to usurp authority; if asked by men to be silent, they should be. However, Philip's daughters were effective, in Acts 21:9, in prophesying. Women are vital in the ministry with other women, children, and even on occasion in leadership when no Christian men take leadership (such as Lydia in Acts who started the Philippian church in her home). We know later, by reading Philippians, that men took over the leadership, but we can rest assured that Lydia prayed, served, and taught faithfully, as do the women and evangelical-like women missionaries of today, and the Priscillas of the New Testament.

Explanation of Passages Used by Charismatics to Justify Their Divisive Doctrines

The first principle is that all of these passages are to be studied in light of their context. When you do so, you'll note that all have qualifying statements.

- ✦ 1 Corinthians 14:5—"I would that ye all speak with tongues." Used correctly in that day, as tongues was a tool used as a sign to reach the Jews, but Paul immediately qualifies it and says, "[I would] rather that ye prophesied." It is so much more important to communicate clearly the teachings of the Lord than to produce a sign that validates but does not teach.

- ✦ 1 Corinthians 14:18—Paul says, "I thank my God, I speak with tongues more than ye all," yet he immediately qualifies it with "yet ... I would rather speak five words with my understanding." In all of Paul's ministry and in all the other epistles he wrote to churches all over the known world, he never refers to tongues or uses them in his ministry. His only reference is to this carnal, immature church.

- ✦ 1 Corinthians 14:39—"Forbid not to speak with tongues" (explained previously, as were 14:4, 12:31, and 14:1).

Exposition of Passages in Acts in Which Tongues Are Mentioned

ACTS 2:1-21:

- ✦ This is the beginning of the dispensation of the church, which is distinctive from all other dispensations for many reasons. A prominent one is the unique work of the Holy Spirit in the lives of believers.

- ✦ Pentecost is the official introduction of the Holy Spirit, as promised in John 7:37-39 and 14:16-26, as the "paraclete" (counselor) who will indwell every believer and glorify Christ through the believer by conforming the believer to the image of Christ (Romans 8:29).

❧ The purpose of the Holy Spirit in the world is to glorify Christ; consequently, the manifestation of tongues in Acts 2 conforms to the concept of communication, even as the wind denotes power and fire denotes that an individual filled by the Spirit is a light in the world (Acts 2:3, 4).

❧ All believers present were filled with the Spirit (2:4). Although in this instance the filling and baptism happened at the same time, they are not synonymous, but two distinct ministries of the Spirit. For a believer there is only one baptism (1 Corinthians 12:12, 13; 1 John 2:20, 27), but many fillings with the Spirit (Acts 2:4, 4:29-31; Ephesians 1:13, 14, 5:18). Study the differences between baptism, indwelling, sealing, and filling of and by the Spirit.

❧ Known tongues and a desire to communicate the Gospel are the result of filling by the Spirit. To be filled with the Spirit is to have the tools necessary to accomplish the job that God has given you to do. In this case, foreign tongues were necessary to preach the message to the many Jewish foreigners and to fulfill the prophecies of Joel 2:28-32 and Isaiah 28:11, 12; tongues is a sign gift to the Jews (Acts 2:5-12).

❧ Three thousand were saved that day, but no mention of anyone of them speaking in tongues, even though they grew steadfastly in doctrine (2:41). Tongues were a sign gift to the 120, and were not a part of the 3,000 though they were in "one accord" and many others were saved (2:41-47).

Acts 10:44-48:

❧ Great controversy in beginning of church age as to whether gentiles were to be a part of the church.

❧ God wanted to make this clear to Jews that Bride is for anyone—Jew, Greek, or otherwise—and brings to pass this "gentile Pentecost." The same thing happened to these gentiles as happened to the Jews (note Acts 10:47 and 11:15). The tongues were a sign to the Jews that the Gospel was to go to the gentiles also. There were many other instances in

Acts in which people were saved without manifestation of tongues; here, it was a sign of God's confirmation that gentiles get the Gospel, too.

ACTS 19:1-7:

- A hard passage unless we apply the interpretation principles.

- Again a sign to the Jews, many of whom had believed John's prophet-like message of "repent, for the kingdom is at hand." Many Jews believed in John's message and looked forward to the restoration of Israel in power, as prophesied by the prophets. Sad to say, they were not in the majority, nor did their leaders believe John's message or even Christ's kingdom message at the beginning of His ministry. These twelve men were devout men who followed John but had not yet heard the message of Christ.

- That they were devout is proved by their readiness to accept Christ (19:5).

- In the presence of these Jews, and undoubtedly others around him, Paul laid hands on them and, as in the Jewish and gentile Pentecosts, they burst forth in languages they had never known before but which the listeners understood.

- This sign confirmed to the Jews that John's prophet-like message has been superseded by the Gospel of grace.

OTHER:

- The only other questionable passage concerning the Holy Spirit coming after the initial act of salvation is Acts 8:15-17. Tongues are not mentioned here but implied.

- Again we know that Samaritans were hated by Jews (John 4); for the Gospel to go to them was a real dilemma to the Jews. Remember, this was even before the gentile Pentecost of Acts 10.

- In Acts 1:8, Christ had specified Jerusalem: Jews, Judea, Samaria—Samarians, and uttermost parts of the earth— gentiles, and now it was upon them. Should they take the Samaritans in as a part of the church? They had not been accepted into orthodox Jewish religion.

⋗ God said yes and confirmed it in the same way as the Jewish Pentecost in Acts 2 and later in the gentile Pentecost and for the devout Jews of other lands.

Mistakes in the Present Tongues Movement

⋗ *Speaking in tongues is synonymous with baptism of the Holy Spirit.* To be baptized by the Spirit is to be placed into and identified with the body of Christ. This happens to every believer the moment that person accepts Christ. In 1 Corinthians 12:12-14, we see that all believing Corinthians were baptized into the body even though some, obviously, had not spoken in tongues. Read Acts 11:15-18; Romans 6:1-4; 1 John 2:20-27.

   Some confusion lies in the fact that in some instances baptism and filling both happened at the same time (e.g., the experience of Acts 2 as described in Acts 1:5), but baptism, filling, indwelling, sealing, etc., are all separate functions of the Holy Spirit. All Christians are baptized with the Holy Spirit but absolutely do not speak in tongues.

⋗ *Speaking in tongues is evidence of filling by the Holy Spirit.* Ephesians 5:18 commands the believer to be filled, but not one passage commands to speak in tongues. There were numerous instances when disciples were filled but did not speak in tongues (Acts 4:31; 13:9-11). Evidence of being filled is described in Ephesians 5:18-20 and includes: (1) joyful heart, (2) thankful heart, (3) submissive heart—but nothing is said about tongues. We are to be like Christ, yet we never see Christ speaking in tongues, nor do many great men of God today and in the past. To be filled is to be under the control of and submissive to the Spirit—that's all.

⋗ *Speaking in tongues is the fruit of the Spirit.* It is a gift, not fruit (1 Corinthians 13). Fruit comes as a result of being filled. Galatians 5:23 never lists tongues as a fruit, nor does any other passage. John 10:41, 42 declares John the Baptist's power, and Christ called him greatest, but he never spoke in tongues. Best evidence of filling is quality of life, not tongues.

- *Speaking in tongues shows evidence of faith.* Just the opposite. Tongue seekers remind us of the Jews who were always seeking confirmatory signs (Thomas; John 20:24-29). We are to walk by faith and not by sight; we are to believe God's Word and promises without confirmatory signs like those needed before the canon was completed.

- *All are to seek gift of tongues.* Not all are to have tongues (1 Corinthians 12:4-11). The Holy Spirit assigns gifts (1 Corinthians 12:11). They are given at new birth, and it is not up to us to choose. Also, tongues are not that important: read 1 Corinthians 14, where tongues are last in every list. Even the self-edification of 1 Corinthians 14:4 is called selfish in 14:12, where we are told to live to edify the church, not ourselves.

- *Encouraging women speaking in church.* This is clearly contrary to 1 Corinthians 14:34, 35. 1 Corinthians 11:5 teaches that a woman can minister under certain restrictions, but is never to usurp authority over men (1 Timothy 2:9-15).

- *Assuming that sign gifts are for believers today.* God does work miracles and healings today, but not through individuals who have these special gifts. The temporary gifts were given only until the Bible was completed. The Holy Spirit illuminates the Bible and miraculously makes it clear, to those who read with open hearts, that until the Bible was complete God gave the temporary gifts to validate certain persons (apostles and prophets) as authoritative. Now the Bible is our authority (1 Corinthians 13:8-10) and temporary gifts are not necessary, because the Bible is complete. Tongues were called a sign gift clearer than any other (1 Corinthians 14:22), and were given as a special function during the transitional period.

- Other problems:
  - Charismatics place more value on tongues than they should (1 Corinthians 14).
  - Emphasizes that gifts are acquired after salvation; implies that God is our debtor, that He owes us some special gifts.

Further implies that He withholds a special gift until we beg, grovel, and promise in a legalistic subjection. This is contrary to love, grace, and the fellowship we are to enjoy in liberty.

- People have become unhappy and wretched in honest effort to speak in tongues.
- Causes divisions like no other movement; hurts body truth and unity.
- Spiritual frustration and even gross carnality result from modern tongues movement.
- Women are misused and misinformed. Satan tempted Eve. Note damsel in Acts 16:16-18, "spirit of divination." They are tender and susceptible.
- Tongues in a public meeting repel the unsaved (1 Corinthians 14:23-25).
- Fail to recognize tongues as worthless in an assembly today (1 Corinthians 14:5-19).
- Evangelism and preaching/teaching of the Word are subverted to quest for and use of tongues in the typical charismatic meeting.
- Implies that possession of gifts signifies spirituality.
- Encourages pride and fleshly striving instead of Scriptural resting, growing, and depending.
- Promotes false doctrine, such as possible loss of salvation. (The ultimate sanctification in this life is dissolving of old sinful nature).
- Does not rightly divine Word.
- Discourages open study of Word.
- Doesn't recognize that some gifts were temporary.
- Encourages self-edification rather than church edification.
- Constantly breaks rules of 1 Corinthians 14:27-39.
- Ignores behest that if there is no interpreter, keep silent.
- Ignores instruction that only two or three are to speak, and then one at a time.
- Women are not silent, are often indecent in their gyrations and lack of control, and are not submissive on many occasions.

- Ecumenical—no separation. Liberals, moderns, and Roman Catholics are all involved with evangelicals in the charismatic movement today. Scriptural doctrine is stunted if common experience is occurring.
- Makes experience more important and authoritative than Scripture.
- Childish in outlook and actions. Resistant to any other teaching, regardless of verification by Scripture.
- Very shallow—do not understand vital doctrines of soteriology, eschatology, etc.
- Because they are so experience-oriented, charismatics talk down men of God who are students of Bible, language, etc., and emphasize their personal experience.

How Do We Explain Present-Day Speaking in Tongues?

There are really only three options regarding present-day tongues:

- Present-day tongues are Scriptural and a special gift still in use today. We reject this on the basis of all of our study previously presented.

- Present-day tongues are self-induced, either by individuals or by groups in a sort of group hysteria. We feel this is an explanation for many of the experiences of charismatic groups and individuals of today. Many, though totally sincere, are completely ignorant of Scriptural doctrine, and work themselves into terrible frenzies, like the priests of Baal on Mt. Carmel in Elijah's day and the heathen cults in primitive tribes today and heathen cultures of yesterday.

- Present-day tongues are satanically induced. This too is Scriptural, as one of Satan's great tools is infiltration (witness the golden calf, Nehemiah's foes, Gibeonites, sons of God in Genesis 6 and many other passages). Satan is very cunning and would divide believers and cause them to be occupied with anything but the Bible and winning others. We also know that he uses miracles to deceive, as in Pharaoh's court, and in these last days through the antichrist as described in 2 Thessalonians 2:9-12: "signs," tongues, and "lying wonders," including counterfeit healing that is nothing more than removal of indwelling demons. This is the strong delusion of verse 11. There are many instances in Scripture where Satan took control of the vocal cords of both animals and people (Baalam, man at Gadera, etc.).

In short, we are to avoid tongues and those who seek them (Romans 16:17, 18)!

Summary of Teaching on Tongues

- ✺ Tongues was a legitimate gift temporarily given as a sign to validate the authority of the speaker and to use as a sign to the Jews until the canon was completed. Actually, it was a warning to the Jews that the sixth cycle of discipline was imminent.

- ✺ Tongues were a known tongue or a foreign language, often not known by the speaker but understood by another, who was to interpret to other believers present.

- ✺ Tongues was least important of spiritual gifts.

- ✺ Tongues was most misused gift, as described in 1 Corinthians 12-14.

- ✺ Tongues do not indicate that exerciser is spiritual, filled, sanctified, or any special person in God's plan.

- ✺ Tongues were not to be sought after, and were not to be enjoyed by every believer, as there are diversities of gifts.

- ✺ The better way of getting God's work done is through administration of the gifts of love.

- ✺ Prophecy or communication of the Word is much more important than charismatic tongues.

- ✺ Present-day tongues are either self- or group-induced or satanically induced.

- ✺ We are to separate from those who teach and seek tongues.

Anthropology
Doctrine of Man

❧❧

INTRODUCTION

The term *anthropology* is derived from the Greek word that means "man," *anthropos*. It is the science of man. It is very important for the believer to study this subject, as it is probably the most controversial area in theology as far as the unsaved world is concerned. The approach to this subject comes from two divergent angles: the wide, popular angle of the world, which ignores or denies the existence and power of a personal, sovereign God; and from the narrow, less accepted Biblical and Christian viewpoint, which contends that God originated man as the highest being in the universe, and that man was created with purpose in one complete act.

Anthropology deals with all that enters into man's being, both material and immaterial: his origin, nature, reason for existence, variances in existence, destiny, relationship—in essence, all human experience and expression. This encompasses much. It is natural that man, existing with reason, would seek to understand his origin, yet man cannot ever discover his origin without revelation from God. He cannot discover his origin unaided; he can only surmise and speculate. Only saved men can understand and believe the Biblical revelations considering man's origin (Matthew 11:27-29), which is clearly explained in Genesis 1-3, Colossians 1:16, and

Hebrews 11:3, as well as in many facets of theology that explain a God of purpose, design, and power.

I. THE ORIGIN OF MAN

In modern, Christless scholarship, nothing is more scoffed at than the Biblical account of creation as put forth in Genesis. This disdain is carried into many areas of science, philosophy, and history, and it is a basic difference between the believer who is able to believe God's revelation by faith and the unbeliever who is not. This is explained in 1 Corinthians 2:9-16. There are really two general classes of people so far as ideas on man's origin is concerned: (1) those who believe Biblical records, and (2) those who do not. When you become a believer, every area of knowledge changes, because the believer's basic foundation of knowledge is the existence of a personal God who made humanity for a special purpose. The unbeliever is forced to look upon the earth and humankind as an accident and, consequently, without reason, logic, or purpose in existence. Therefore, the science, philosophy, and history of unbelievers must vary from Scriptural concepts. This variance makes the study of anthropology critical for believers.

Summary of Positions Concerning the Origin of Man

- *Atheists* say there is no God, so they are forced to accept evolution, or some modification thereof, which posits that humanity arose from natural developments.

- *Agnostics* claim that man cannot know God, thereby declaring their lack of trust in the Bible, and thus argue that no one can know for certain about man's origin. They feel that humanity could have come into existence by spontaneous generation (*abiogenesis*)—that is, by accident, without a cause. They may also be evolutionists.

- *Evolutionists,* who hold many and varied opinions, claim that man came into existence by slowly developing from nothing to his present state. Variances arise because of differences in theories as to the beginning of life, the organization of that matter, and the time it took to bring civilization to its present state. Some type of evolutionary view is held by atheists, agnostics, and even some theists.

✺ *Theistic evolutionists* wish to harmonize science and the Bible, and claim that the proofs of the earth's great age are indisputable. Therefore, they endeavor to show there was a great gap of time, or a number of gaps, between events recorded in the first few verses of Genesis. This is known as the "gap theory," and it argues that the six "days" of Genesis are great blocks of time rather than twenty-four-hour periods.

✺ *Intelligent design (ID)* is a teleological argument for the existence of God,[1] stated in allegedly secular terms, based on the premise that "certain features of the universe and of living things are best explained by an intelligent cause, not an undirected process such as natural selection."[2] Its leading proponents, all of whom are affiliated with the Discovery Institute,[3] claim that intelligent design is a scientific theory

---

1. "ID is not a new scientific argument, but is rather an old religious argument for the existence of God. He traced this argument back to at least Thomas Aquinas in the 13th century, who framed the argument as a syllogism: Wherever complex design exists, there must have been a designer; nature is complex; therefore nature must have had an intelligent designer" (known as the *teleological argument*). *Kitzmiller v. Dover Area School District*, 04-CV-2688, 2005 WL 578974 (M.D. Pa., December 20, 2005).

2. *FAQs: Questions about Intelligent Design* (Discovery Institute, Center for Science and Culture, n.d.), available at http://www.discovery.org/csc/. See also *Primer: Intelligent Design Theory in a Nutshell* (Intelligent Design and Evolution Awareness (IDEA), n.d.), available at http://www.ideacenter.org/; "Intelligent Design" (Intelligent Design network, n.d.), available at http://www.intelligentdesignnetwork.org/.

3. See Jodi Wilgoren, "Politicized Scholars Put Evolution on the Defensive," *New York Times*, August 21, 2005; "Who Is Behind the ID Movement?," available at http://www.aclu.org/religion/schools/16371res20050916.html; Discovery Institute, http://www.discovery.org; Joseph P. Kahn, "The Evolution of George Gilder," *Boston Globe*, July 27, 2005; "Who's Who of Intelligent Design Proponents," available at http://www.discovery.org/scripts/viewDB/filesDB-download.php?command=download&id=602; American Association for the Advancement of Science, "Intelligent Design and Peer Review" (n.d.), available at http://www.aaas.org/spp/dser/03_Areas/evolution/issues/peerreview.shtml; Alan Attie et al., "Defending Science Education against Intelligent Design: A Call to Action," *Journal of Clinical Investigation* 116 (2006):1134–38, available at http://www.jci.org/cgi/content/full/116/5/1134.

that stands on equal footing with, or is superior to, current scientific theories regarding the evolution and origin of life.[4]

◦ *Creationists* take the Biblical account of creation, as described in Genesis 1, 2, as literal; they regard the days referenced therein as twenty-four-hour days, at least from Genesis 1:3 on. Of course, we cannot be dogmatic on the true age of the earth, because we do not have information on when God created the universe as described in Genesis 1:1 and when God started the work in Genesis 1:3; however, we are not to assume that there was evolution, as opposed to static existence, during the time of Genesis 1:1, 2.

Also, we do not know how long Adam and Eve lived in the Garden of Eden in their state of innocence, so it is not wise for anyone to date the earth. In adding up genealogies from the birth of Seth, we can account for 6,000 to 12,000 years (variances are possible because of evident gaps, overlapping, and the varied use and meaning of the term *son* in Scripture).

To summarize, we state that God has given us sufficient information to recognize that He planned and created the earth as it is to His glory. Many details were left out because God deemed them unimportant to the total concept that He desired: namely, that God made the universe, world, and man to His own glory. In faith we accept His account and leave the details up to God.

Summary of the Scriptural Account of Man's Origin

◦ Scriptural testimony (Genesis 1, 2; Exodus 20:11; Psalms 33:6, 9; Nehemiah 9:6; 2 Peter 3:5; Hebrews 4:3, 10).

◦ Creationists believe in six twenty-four-hour days, as mentioned in Exodus 20:11.

◦ "Evening and morning" is a qualifying phrase—numerical adjectives.

---

4. Stephen C. Meyer, *The Scientific Status of Intelligent Design: The Methodological Equivalence of Naturalistic and Non-Naturalistic Origins Theories* (Ignatius Press, 2005); see also Michael Behe, *Darwin's Black Box* (Free Press, 1996).

ᴥ "Our image ... our likeness" (Genesis 1:26) shows how God's unique creation of man explains difference of man from animals. Living soul (Genesis 2:7).

Theistic Evolution

How, then, do we explain rock strata, dinosaurs, fossils, and ancient men? Two ways:

ᴥ Dr. Bernard Northrup claims to have proven that all geologic features could have come into existence or occurred in 6,000 to 10,000 years, especially during the time of the Flood (see Northrup, "Taphonomy: A Tool for Studying Earth's Biblical History" (revised January 1997), available at http://www.ldolphin.org/taphon.html.

ᴥ Dr. Morris and Dr. Whitcomb and associates (see John C. Whitcomb and Henry M. Morris, *The Genesis Flood* (P & R Publishing, 1989)) claim:

 ᴥ Earth created with age—Adam (miraculous example of Christ making wine out of water).

 ᴥ Great catastrophe came to create fossils; sudden death, pressure, temperature, glacier all too slow. This was the Flood followed by freeze—greenhouse effect. Half water above firmament (Genesis 1:6).

 ᴥ Mountains covered at least 15 cubits (Psalms 104:6-9; Job 15:7); Himalayas are 26,000 feet.

 ᴥ Creationist explanation of dinosaurs, fossils, glaciers, strata, etc., is that the whole earth prior to Flood was a greenhouse with heat held by special firmament. Flood released water, haze disappeared, and suddenly poles became ice. Sudden temperature change caused upheaval of mountains and valleys, glaciers and hot weather; vegetarian animals like dinosaurs died; seasons started (Genesis 8:12), and no flood would come again because firmament was emptied. Fossils only come with sudden death, great upheaval and pressure—only explanation for fossils which, in many cases, were pre-Flood animals. Canyons formed by great Flood runoff.

Problems with Theistic Evolution

- Current language study indicates that words in original do not justify translating *bara* as "become." Original words can no longer be used as a valid argument for putting great expanses of time into Genesis 1, 2.

- Problems arise with order of creation as described in Bible. Example: third day, fruit trees and grass after marine life; or earth first, then moon and stars, insects that pollinate after fruit trees, flowers, or plants before sun. Evolutionary order is different.

- Theistic evolutionists are dying out. They were very strong in the 1940s and 1950s but science and Scripture have proven many of their hypotheses unacceptable.

Reasons for Opposing Evolution

Evolution is anti-Scriptural for many reasons:

- Denies power of God.

- Denies personal God.

- Denies Fall of man and introduction of sin; consequently, denies necessity of redemption of humanity.

- Denies special creation of man with a soul and spirit.

- Denies purpose of future hope for humanity.

- Denies veracity of and need for Bible, which deals with redemption and eschatology. If evolutionary theory is correct, humanity has no hope.

- Does not acknowledge inconsistency in recognizing marvels of creation and yet teaching that it all came into existence by chance. Example: science of heredity shows similarities of like entities being consistently passed on, while blood of man, animals, and fish are different, as are their respective flesh and makeup.

- Scripture says "after his kind," and that man was created in God's image for a purpose (Genesis 1, 2). There is no record of animal becoming man; if so, there would be living examples today, and Scripture would confirm such a dramatic occurrence. In fact, Scripture very clearly points out the difference between men and animals in Genesis 1:26, in the recommendation of animals and fish for food (clean animals, fishing, etc.) and in the prohibition on bestiality, etc.

ﾟ Every piece of evidence of evolution of animals given by scientists consists of instances within a species (which a creationist doesn't deny). There is no evidence of "crossover" evolution in which one species becomes another species. The Bible says, "after its own kind."

ﾟ Carbon-14, once used to prove age, is now known to have a half-life of only 5,760 years. This dating technique is most accurate in specimens that have been dead for much shorter periods than that. To explain: All living things take in carbon-14 from the air (plants) and food (animals) and the ratio of carbon-14 to carbon-12 remains at the same level throughout life. At death, carbon-14 ceases to enter the object but begins to decay, while carbon-12 remains stable; thus, by measuring the ratio of carbon-14 to carbon-12, one can determine how long something has been dead. This system is not accurate over long time spans and yields some variances even in shorter periods.

ﾟ Lack of consistency among scholars of evolution (hoax of Piltdown man; Java man, Neanderthals).

The Laws of Thermodynamics

ﾟ First law of thermodynamics states that all energy is conserved, and the amount of energy within our universe remains stable (that is, in any process, the total energy of the universe remains constant). To a Christian, this is easily understood, as we recognize that God produced the universe in a complete, single sequence of events over a span of time in the beginning and then ceased and rested on the seventh day. There has been no addition of energy or matter since the beginning (Colossians 1:16, 17; Hebrews 1:2, 3; 2 Peter 3:5-7; Psalms 148:5, 6; Isaiah 40:26; Ecclesiastes 1:9-10, 2:14, 15).

✵ The second law states there is a universal principle of change in nature which is "downhill," not "uphill" as evolution requires: In any spontaneous physical change, entropy always increases. (*Entropy* is a measure of the quantity of energy not capable of conversion into work.) Stephen Hawking described this using time as an entropy base. For example, time moves in a forward direction, so when one breaks a cup of coffee on the floor, no matter what happens, in our universe, one will never see the cup re-form. Cups are breaking all the time, but never re-forming. Since the Big Bang, the entropy (disorder) of the universe has been on the rise; the second law states that this process will continue to increase (see http://en.wikipedia.org/wiki/Second_law_of_thermodynamics) (Psalms 102:25-27; Isaiah 51:6; 1 Peter 1:24, 25; Hebrews 12:27; Romans 7:21-25; Revelation 21:4; 22:3).

II. The Nature of Man

Original Image of Man

✵ Man is made in God's image (Genesis 1:26, 9:6; 1 Corinthians 11:7; James 3:9).

✵ Like God is man's triunity of body, soul, and spirit—man is trichotomous (Genesis 2:17; Matthew 8:22; Ephesians 2:5; 2 Corinthians 5:17; 1 Thessalonians 5:23; Hebrews 4:12). Some teach that man is dichotomous prior to salvation and trichotomous after salvation. This is metaphorically true in practice, but man is still above the animals and unsaved man is referred to as having a spirit, though that spirit is often described as evil (Deuteronomy 2:30; 1 Chronicles 5:26; 2 Chronicles 36:22, etc.). More accurate is the view that the unsaved man has a trichotomous nature, but his spirit is dead to the Lord's spirit, as described in 2 Corinthians 2.

✵ Man is like God in his intellectual and moral nature (Colossians 3:9-10; Ephesians 4:24).

- Man is like God in his manifested physical likeness; true God is a spirit (John 4:24) and invisible (Colossians 1:15), but Christ became a man who was express image of God (Hebrews 1:3).

- Original man was innocent. This does not mean holy or righteous. *Innocence* is sinlessness that has never faced trial. *Righteousness* is innocence that has been tested and tried and come out victorious.

Constitution of Man

Body

- Made from the earth and given life by God (Genesis 2:7). It is the house of the inner man (Job 4:19; 2 Corinthians 5:1, 3, 4). That the body consists of the same elements as dust is verified by chemical analysis and the fact that earth sustains man and man turns to dust in death.

Soul

- God gave man a soul (Genesis 2:7; 1 Corinthians 15:45).

- The soul is the seat of emotions and appetites. It seems that plants, animals, and men have bodies, that animals and men have souls, but that only man has a spirit. The difference between man's soul and an animal's soul is that an animal's soul is connected to the body, whereas the soul of man is connected to his spirit.

- Basically the soul is made up of six facets:
  - Self-consciousness (Genesis 35:18; 1 Kings 17:21; Matthew 10:39; Acts 20:10).
  - Mentality (Luke 12:9; Ephesians 4:18; Psalms 59:12).
  - Volition, also known as free will (Acts 3:23 [Adam in Garden]).
  - Emotion (Song of Solomon 1:7; Luke 12:19; John 12:27; 2 Peter 2:8).
  - Conscience (Acts 24:16; Romans 2:15, 9:1, 2).

↝ Old sin nature (Leviticus 5:1; Psalms 58:2-5; Ezekiel 18:4; Jeremiah 17:9; Matthew 15:19).

↝ Other facets and attributes of the soul are many:
  ↝ Desires (1 Samuel 2:16; Deuteronomy 12:20; Psalms 107:18; Proverbs 6:30).
  ↝ Hates (2 Samuel 5:8).
  ↝ Mourns (Job 14:22).
  ↝ Is vexed (2 Kings 4:27).
  ↝ Rejoices (Isaiah 61:10).
  ↝ Suffers (Genesis 42:21).

↝ Where does man get his soul? Three theories:
  ↝ Preexistence—all souls were created in beginning and at time of conception are united with body.
  ↝ Creationism—forty days after conception, soul unites with body (Roman Catholic).
  ↝ Traducionism—both body and soul are derived from parents (Genesis 5:3; Acts 17:24-26; Exodus 21:22-23; Psalms 51:5, 139:13; Luke 1:41-44).

Spirit—Where Man Differs from All Creatures

↝ Source is God (Hebrews 12:9: "Father of the spirits").

↝ Unsaved have spirit (Genesis 41:8; Ezekiel 13:3; Daniel 2:1; Zechariah 12:1).

↝ Seat of intelligence (1 Corinthians 2:11).

↝ Word *spirit* in both Hebrew and Greek is sometimes translated "breath" or "wind." Context determines translation; this is why materialists say *spirit* should be translated as "breath" and believe that when man dies, he is gone forever.

Special Notes

↝ Soul connotes immaterial part of man related to life such as emotion, action, etc. Words *soma* and *sarkz* are interchangeable.

- Spirit is that part related to worship, communion, divine influence. Words *pneuma* and *psuche* are interchangeable (1 Corinthians 2).

- *Heart* means various things depending on context, such as "old sin nature," "seat of conscience"; *mind* often refers to new man (Romans 7:25).

III. THE HISTORY OF MAN ON EARTH AFTER HIS CREATION

Condition before the Fall (Genesis 2:7-25)

- His home: God made Eden, east of Jerusalem, for man (Genesis 2:8).

- Eden's description:
  - Every tree pleasant to sight and good for food.
  - Two other trees: life and knowledge of good and evil; man needs these also.
  - A river for water—complete provision.

- His work: man was to work—"till it and keep it" (Genesis 2:15).

- His food: freely eat of every tree—grace, but not of tree of knowledge, lest you die.

- His knowledge (2:18-20).
  - God created every beast and brought them unto Adam (2:19).
  - "To see what he would call them"—tremendous amount and infinite names.

- His fellowship with God (2:19, 3:8) and companionship with Eve (2:20-25).

- His responsibility:
  - To replenish the earth (1:28, 3:20).
  - To abstain from eating of the fruit—God wanted to give men knowledge but not through disobedience. Faith is to trust God to give us all we need, including knowledge-wise and in every other realm (physical, spiritual, etc.).

Fall of Man (Genesis 3:1-24)

The Source of Sin

- The serpent who was the vehicle of Satan or Satan himself—
  he was not identified in Genesis, but we know Satan was
  tempter (2 Corinthians 11:3; 1 Timothy 2:14); called serpent
  in Revelation 12:9.
- Original sin in universe described in Isaiah 14:12-17 and
  Ezekiel 28:1-19.

The Nature of Sin

- "Hath God said?" (3:1). Questioning God's grace,
  implication that God was holding back something that was
  good.
- Eve left out words "freely" and "surely" in 3:2. Man's
  tendency is to leave out revelation and Satan seized on the
  last word "surely" in Genesis 3:4 (2:16, 17).
- Satan lied (3:5).
- Man's doubts brought about his downfall:
  - Doubted God's love (Proverbs 14:12).
  - Doubted God's Word (1 John 3:4).
  - Doubted God's authority (Romans 8:7, 8).
- Familiar pattern of temptation and fall (1 John 2:16;
  Genesis 3:6).
  - "Saw"—looked to investigate.
  - "Good for food"—"lust of flesh."
  - "Pleasant to the eyes"—"lust of eyes."
  - "Make one wise"—"pride of life." Same pattern in
    temptation of Christ (Matthew 4:1-11; Mark 2:12, 13;
    Luke 4:1-13).
- Adam followed Eve's example although he was not deceived
  (1 Timothy 2:14).

Effects of Sin

IMMEDIATE EFFECTS:

- Shame (Genesis 2:25, 3:7).
- Fear—"I was afraid" (3:10).
- Separation from God—"hid" (3:10).
- Expulsion from Garden (3:23, 24).
- Lost lordship over creation.

FAR-REACHING EFFECTS:

- Spirit darkened (Ephesians 4:17, 18).
- Soul debased, corrupt (Ephesians 4:19).
- Body subjected to disease and death (Romans 8:21).

IMMEDIATE EFFECTS ON SUBJECTS:

- Serpent (Genesis 3:14, 15).
- Woman (Genesis 3:16).
- Man (Genesis 5:29).
- Creation (Genesis 3:17, 18).

FUTURE EFFECTS:

- Man is lost and condemned to hell (Revelation 21:8).
- God's provision for man (3:15, 21; John 3:16).

STATE OF THE SINNER:

- In first Adam—lost (1 Corinthians 15:21, 22, 45:47; Romans 5:12-21; exposition of Romans 1-3).
  - Sinful in nature (Psalms 51:5; Ephesians 2:3).
  - Sinful in practice (Titus 3:3; Romans 3:23; Colossians 1:21; Psalms 14:1-3).
  - Spiritually dead (Ephesians 2:1, 5).
  - Under God's wrath (Romans 1:18; John 3:36).
  - Waits for death (Hebrews 9:27).
  - Sure of hell (Revelation 20:15).

- In second Adam—saved (1 Corinthians 15:21, 22, 45, 47; Romans 5:12-21). Perfect in position (Ephesians 1:4, 6).

- His state as a new creature (2 Corinthians 5:17).
  - Saved (2 Timothy 1:9; Ephesians 2:8, 9).
  - Dead unto sin (Romans 6:11; 2 Peter 2:24).
  - Child of God (Galatians 3:26).
  - Under God's favor (Ephesians 1:3, Romans 5:2).
  - Waits for God and glory (Philippians 3:20, 21).
  - Sure of Heaven (2 Timothy 4:18; 1 Peter 1:4).

Man's Two Natures

Many of these points are drawn from Cambron's *Bible Doctrines* (1954).

- Household of Abraham (Galatians 5:17): Ishmael—flesh, Isaac—spirit. Trouble arose when Isaac came into household.

- Names and characteristics of new nature are:
  - Spirit (John 3:6).
  - Divine nature (2 Peter 1:4; 1 John 3:9, 5:18, 19).
  - New man (Ephesians 4:24; Colossians 3:10; 2 Corinthians 5:17).
  - Inward man (2 Corinthians 4:16; Romans 7:22).
  - Mind (Romans 7:25).
  - It is a Christlike nature—imparted, holy, unchangeable, and unending.
  - Its end is resurrection and rapture.

- Names and characteristics of old nature are:
  - Flesh (John 3:6; Romans 7:18, 23, 8:9).
  - Natural man (1 Corinthians 2:14).
  - Old man (Romans 6:6; Colossians 3:9).
  - Outward man (2 Corinthians 4:16).
  - Heart (Mark 7:21-23).
  - Carnal mind (Romans 8:7).
  - Sin (Romans 5:12).
  - It is evil (Romans 8), unchangeable (John 3:6), and its end is death (Romans 6:23).

Conflict between the Two Natures

- As experienced by the believer (Romans 7:15-25; Galatians 5:17).

- Believer's responsibility in relation to the old nature:
  - Accept God's estimate of it (Romans 6:6-11). It is not declared to be crucified in believer but with Christ.
  - Make no provision for flesh; that is, do not feed it—starve it (Romans 13:14).
  - Mortify the flesh (Colossians 3:5; Hebrews 11:12).
  - Don't try to improve it (Romans 6:13).
  - Put it off (Ephesians 4:22).

- Believer's responsibility in relation to new nature:
  - Reckon ourselves to be alive (Romans 6:11).
  - Walk in newness of life (Romans 6:14, 7:6).
  - Feed and nourish it (1 Peter 2:2).
  - Put on new man (Ephesians 4:24).
  - Depend on indwelling Spirit for power (Ephesians 4:30, 6:10; Zechariah 4:6b).

Harmartiology
Doctrine of Sin

❧♨❧

INTRODUCTION

In the study of anthropology, we studied the Fall of man. This included teachings on the introduction of sin into the universe through Satan's jealousy of God (Isaiah 14; Ezekiel 28), and into the world in the Garden of Eden (Genesis 3).

We now look at the details of sin as taught in Scripture. Throughout, our goals are to reinforce, first, God's hatred of and incompatibility with sin, and second, the fact that God's righteousness and justice demand that man's sin be reconciled before man can have fellowship with God in any matter.

- Sin is never to be treated lightly, for it cost God much to effect man's reconciliation.

- Sin is never to be treated lightly, because it will destroy those who do so both in this life and for eternity.

- Sin will ultimately be conquered and disappear.

We intend a refutation of philosophers and teachers who regard sin as something less than the Biblical standard and definition of *sin*. There are various types of rejecters of these Biblical standards, ranging from:

- Those who call sin an illusion, based on the misconception that there is no absolute right or wrong. These people hold that all is relative and society and culture decide what is sin and what is not.

- ✣ The gnostic, who regards sin as an opposite principle to God.

- ✣ The ascetic, who believes that sin is material and denies himself while not taking into account spiritual, non-material sin.

- ✣ The epicurean, who indulges his body and physical pleasures.

All of these are in essence denials that man is really a sinner and accountable to God, as the Bible teaches. It is this Scripture-based view of sin that we now investigate.

I. THE REALITY OF SIN

- ✣ Scripture declares the fact of sin. It does exist! (Romans 3:23; Galatians 3:22—"The scripture hath concluded all under sin").

- ✣ Nature also proclaims the fact of sin (Romans 8:22—"We know that the whole creation groaneth and travaileth together in pain").

- ✣ Experience proves the fact of sin—Moses, David, Peter, and John.

II. NONSCRIPTURAL ATTEMPTS TO EXPLAIN SIN

- ✣ Evolutionists say it is a trait of beasts.

- ✣ Psychiatrists vary, but many call it natural inclination and therefore excusable, or merely a weakness.

- ✣ Scholars call it ignorance.

- ✣ Social workers call it lack of education, lack of opportunity, or bad environment.

- ✣ Society calls it indiscretion, intolerance, or legitimate behavior, depending on circumstances.

- ✣ New theologians call it merely selfishness or self-love.

❧ Christian Science teaches that it is absence of good.

III. The Scriptural View of Sin

❧ One can list Scriptural terms describing sin (see Cambron, 1954):
  - 2 Thessalonians 2.
  - "Missing the mark" (Romans 3:23, 5:12).
  - "Transgression"—"Whosoever committeth sin transgresseth also the law: for sin is the transgression of the law" (1 John 3:4).
  - Known or unknown sin; "bending that which is right"—*righteousness* means straight (Romans 1:18, 6:13; 2 Thessalonians 2:12).
  - "Rebellion against God" (Isaiah 1:2; 2 Thessalonians 2:4, 8).
  - "Debt" (Matthew 6:12); "forgive us our debts."
  - "Disobedience" (Ephesians 2:2, 5:6).
  - "Unbelief" (1 John 5:10).
  - "Ungodliness" (Romans 4:5, 5:6).
  - "Iniquity"—wrongdoing to moral order of the universe (Galatians 5:19-21).

❧ Sin is more than selfishness, then. According to Scripture it is:
  - Rebellion toward God (1 Samuel 15:23).
  - Rebellion toward divine law (Numbers 15:30) or ignorance of divine law (Numbers 15:27).
  - Injustice toward man (Leviticus 19:13).
  - Selfishness and corruption toward self (Matthew 16:26; Psalms 51:5).

IV. The Extent and Effects of Sin

❧ To heavens—disrupted them (Ezekiel 38).

❧ To earth—"thorns and thistles" (Genesis 3:17, 18); animals die and fight and are carnivorous (Isaiah 11:6-9).

❧ To humankind (Genesis 3; Romans 3:12, 18, 19, 23).

V. The Penalty for Sin: Death

In Scripture, *death* never means annihilation. There are six deaths:

- Physical—separation of body from soul and spirit; Lazarus.

- Second death—separation from God in eternity (Revelation 20:11-15).

- Scriptural death—separation from God in time—lost! (Romans 5:12).

- Christian positional death—identified in Christ (Galatians 2:20).

- Christian experiential death—loss of fellowship; carnality (Romans 8:6).

- Sexual death—impotence; Abraham (Romans 4:17).

VI. God's Solution to Sin: Christ

- Three major imputations (put on our account) in Scripture (Romans 5:12-18):
  - Imputation of Adam's sin to race—original sin.
  - Imputation of sin of man to Christ—salvation.
  - Imputation of righteousness of God to believer—justification.

- When man accepts Christ:
  - He becomes as righteous as God in his standing (Romans 3:22).
  - At salvation, he becomes two-natured; the old nature still tends to sin, but the new nature, empowered by the Spirit, resists sin and has power over sin. A spiritual conflict rages in the life of the believer who encourages the old sin nature; peace, in this life for the believer, is enjoyed only when the new nature controls that believer's life by submission to the indwelling Holy Spirit.
  - *Carnality* refers to a Christian who is under the control of the old sin nature; it can be rectified by confessing sin to God (1 John 1:9).

VII. THE SERIOUSNESS OF SIN

The import of sin in God's eyes can be seen in many passages. Read Lamentations and see what God did, finally, to a nation that sinned before Him.

Soteriology
Doctrine of Salvation

❧⊰⊱❧

INTRODUCTION

In this chapter we will be studying what is considered by many to be the most important doctrine of Scripture. Many others are also important, but their importance derives from the promise that God, in grace, provides salvation for humanity. The existence of humanity—and in fact the whole universe—hinges on this promise. Consequently, the doctrine of salvation is key.

There are three reasons why the doctrine of salvation should be mastered by every child of God:

- ❧ Our own personal salvation is the result of God's plan of salvation.

- ❧ It is the one message that God has committed to the believer to proclaim to the world.

- ❧ It alone discloses the full measure of God's love.

We go into a great deal of detail so that each student will recognize the immensity and intricate details of God's plan, including our lostness, God's righteousness, His riches of grace, and the completeness of our salvation for now and eternity. Salvation is much more than a fire escape out of hell; Salvation is of the Lord (Jonah 2:9).

We hope that study will truly open your eyes to our "great salvation," which first was spoken by the Lord and then confirmed unto us by them that heard him (Hebrews 2:3). Our hope is that we come to realize that Christ "gave Himself for us that He might redeem us from all iniquity, and purify unto Himself a people of his own zealous good works" (Titus 2:14).

Before we look at the many facets and blessings of salvation, we should look at a basic, foundational truth concerning this great doctrine. In essence, salvation is God's remedy for sin, and it comes to us from three viewpoints (aspects or tenses):

> *Past tense of salvation.* Salvation is wholly completed; it cannot be embellished or changed. It is done, and the one who believes is saved for eternity (1 Corinthians 1:18; 2 Corinthians 2:15; Ephesians 2:5, 8). It is done for eternity (John 5:24, 10:28, 29; Romans 8:1). It is salvation from the penalty of sin.

> *Present tense of salvation.* Salvation includes release from the reigning power of sin (Romans 6:14, 8:2; 2 Corinthians 3:18; Galatians 2:19, 20; Philippians 1:19, 2:12, 13; 2 Thessalonians 2:13).

> *Future tense of salvation.* Salvation includes the truth that the believer will yet be saved into the full conformity of Christ (Romans 8:29, 13:11; 1 Peter 1:5; 1 John 3:2; Philippians 1:6).

Here is an outline of our study:
    Mechanics leading to salvation—conversion
        Repentance—what is it, according to Scripture?
        Faith—from God, or the fruit of a spiritual man?
    What happened when I became saved? Is there a logical order?
        Regeneration
        Justification
        Sanctification
        Adoption
        Redemption
    Assurance
        Proofs of salvation

I. CONVERSION

We define *conversion* as turning to God. It consists of two elements, repentance and faith, both of which are often misunderstood and need definitions that accord with Scripture.

Repentance

Scripture lays much stress on repentance and the preaching of repentance. It was taught in each dispensation past and present:

- Old Testament prophets (Deuteronomy 30:10; 2 Kings 17:13; Jeremiah 8:6; Ezekiel 14:16; 18:30).
- John the Baptist (Matthew 3:2; Mark 1:15).
- Christ (Matthew 4:17; Luke 13:3, 5).
- The Twelve (Mark 6:12).
  - Peter on the day of Pentecost (Acts 2:38; 3:19).
  - Paul also in Acts 20:21, 26:20.

Dispensational change has not made repentance unnecessary in our day (Acts 17:32 [gentiles]; Hebrews 6:1).

The dictionary definition of *repentance* is: "to turn from sin and resolve to reform one's life" (*Merriam-Webster's Dictionary* (Zane Publishing/Merriam-Webster, 2000)). This is not the Scriptural meaning of *repentance*, though, for it implies that one can amend one's own life or pay for sins, in contradiction of the truth that only Christ's blood can pay for sins. One really cannot stop sinning by his own strength, and to endeavor to do so without

Christ for the purpose of salvation smacks of human works and individual effort to please God; this is totally unacceptable to God.

The Scriptural definition of repentance is intended to bring us to recognize that we are sinners who are hopelessly lost and need salvation from God. The Greek word *metanoia* means "a change of mind"; as Thayer's *Lexicon* (Thayer, 1962) defines *metanoia,* it means the "change of mind of those who have begun to abhor their errors and misdeeds, and have determined to enter upon a better course of life." "True repentance is a change of mind which will lead to a change of action" (Cambron, 1954). Examples are Matthew 21:28, 29; and the prodigal son in Luke 15:11-24. Before anyone can be saved, he must have a change of mind about many things: sin, self, God, Christ, good works, etc.

- What repentance is not:
  - Reformation or turning away from sins. Man cannot totally accomplish this. No man is saved by doing something; no man is saved because he gives up something (that is, works). A man can turn from his sins and still not be a Christian.
  - Contrition, agony in the soul for sin. Many folks in prison are sorry because they were caught or are deprived. In genuine repentance, the sinner will be sorry for his sin. Being sorry is not repentance, but it can lead to repentance.
  - Penance, which is the doing of some act to pay for sin, or a voluntary punishment for sin. This is not acceptable to God: only Christ's blood pays for sin.

- True repentance is:
  - Intellectual—a change of view with regard to sin, God, and self. Knowledge of sin (Romans 3:20; Luke 15:17, 18; Psalms 51:3, 7).
  - Emotional—a change of feeling. One does not laugh at or ignore sin, but rather recognizes that one's sin is confining, enslaving, and sending one to hell. Thus, the sinner changes his mind and his attitude on sin, eternity, etc., and begins to desire pardon (Psalms 51:1, 2; 2 Corinthians 7:9, 10).

- Volitional—turning from sin to God, or from a hopeless state to the Lord; choosing to accept God's way.
- "Repentance is the work of God which results in a change of mind in respect to man's relationship to God. It is neither sorrow nor penance, though penitent sorrow may lead to a change of mind. Repentance is always an element of saving faith" (Cambron, 1954).

Faith

Faith is important—witness the references to it in Scripture (these among many others):

- Saved by faith (Acts 16:31; Ephesians 2:8; Romans 5:1).
- Enriched with the Spirit by faith (Galatians 3:5, 14).
- Sanctified by faith (Acts 26:18).
- Kept by faith (1 Peter 1:5; Romans 11:20; 2 Corinthians 1:24; 1 John 5:4).
- Walk by faith (2 Corinthians 5:7).
- Surmount difficulties by faith (Romans 4:18-21; Hebrews 11:17-19, 27).
- Faith necessary to please God (Hebrews 11:6).
- Unbelief a great sin (John 16:9; Romans 14:23).

It is not easy to formulate a simple and adequate definition of *faith*. For instance, the word *belief* is often substituted, but belief really denotes only the intellectual element of faith. Similarly, *hope* has to do exclusively with the future; hope is desire plus expectation. Faith is more than all of these, so a proper definition should include the totality of Christian doctrine as contained in Scripture. Hebrews 11:1 tells more what faith is in its power, but still does not give a full definition. Faith includes the following elements:

- *Knowledge*, or the intellectual element (Romans 10:17)— belief based on evidence. We know there is a God; therefore, we believe in His existence (Romans 1:19, 20). We need to know the Gospel to believe in Christ (Romans 10:14).

- *Volition,* a necessary component of belief. The intelligence of knowledge leads to acceptance of truth. A man of faith does not call God's revelation about man's lost condition a lie, nor does he call the provision of a Savior unnecessary. He *believes* the veracity of the knowledge and thereby takes the first voluntary step toward salvation.

- *Trust,* which blossoms forth from the element of volition. A person chooses to rely upon the knowledge that Christ is the way to Heaven.

- *Recumbency,* which means relying wholly and solely on Christ for salvation. This often leads to an emotional experience as the individual rests and rejoices in his salvation (Psalms 106:12, 13). An emotional element is often the result of faith, but it must not be treated as the sole characteristic or a result of faith. Those who have an undue amount of emotion tend to backslide and feel the need to be saved over and over again.

II. WHAT HAPPENED WHEN I BECAME SAVED?

Many things happen when a person is saved. Some of these things are visible and immediately observed and recognized; some of them happen to us in the sight of the Lord and later become apparent to men as they study the Word and walk in the Lord. Many are instantaneous at salvation; others, such as sanctification, commence at salvation but continue to progress and develop during the life of the believer. There is no logical order, but we will study these facets of salvation so as to commence to enjoy God's far-reaching and totally satisfying salvation—satisfying both to God and to us.

Regeneration

Regeneration is the emphasis on the new birth. It is the passing from death (spiritual death—separation from God in time—lost) to life. It is being born again or born of God into one who is a new creation (John 3:3, 5; 1 Peter 1:23; 1 John 3:9, 2:29, 5:4, 18). It is the aspect of salvation that deals with our transformation from hopelessness to eternal life by the grace of God. Regeneration deals with salvation from our viewpoint.

It is not:

✤ Reformation.

✤ Water baptism.

✤ Church membership.

✤ The result of taking communion or any other religious ritual.

It is:

✤ The new birth whereby man becomes a new creation (2 Corinthians 5:17; 1 John 2:9).

✤ The communication of divine life to the soul (John 3:5, 10:10, 28; 1 John 5:11, 12). As spoken of in Scripture, the heart, generally, is the soul: the self, or that which thinks and feels, wills, and acts. Regeneration involves the soul.

Regeneration is compulsory for eternal life (John 3:7: "Ye must be born again!"):

✤ Because man is depraved (John 3:6).

✤ Because all men are lost (Romans 3:23).

✤ As seen in holiness of God (1 Peter 1:16).

✤ To provide fellowship with God (John 1:12; 1 John 3:1). By nature, all men are "children of wrath" (Ephesians 2:3) and sons of disobedience (Ephesians 2:2); they are "sons of this age" (Luke 16:8) and "children of the devil" (1 John 3:10; Matthew 13:38, 23:15; Acts 13:10).

The Means or Agencies of Regeneration

✤ The will of God. We are born by the "will of God" (John 1:13).

✤ The death and resurrection of Christ (John 3:14-16; 1 Peter 1:3).

- The Word of God (James 1:18; John 3:5); water of Word (Ephesians 5:26).

- The ministers of the Word (1 Corinthians 4:15; Philemon 10; Galatians 4:19).

- The Holy Spirit (John 3:5, 6; Titus 3:5).

The Results of Regeneration

- One born of God overcomes temptation (1 John 3:9, 5:4, 18).

- He habitually loves brethren (1 John 5:1).

- He habitually loves God (1 John 5:2, 4:19).

- He habitually loves his enemies (Matthew 5:44).

- He habitually loves the Word (Psalms 119:97; 1 Peter 2:2).

- He habitually loves lost souls (2 Corinthians 5:14).

- He enjoys child's privileges—needs supplied (Matthew 7:11); revelation of God's will (1 Corinthians 2:10-12); and of keeping (1 John 5:18).

- He is the heir of God and joining-heir with Christ (Romans 8:16, 17) in the future and the Holy Spirit in time (Ephesians 1:13, 14).

- He exhibits the fruit of the Spirit, as described in Galatians 5:22, 23, and lives a life that is dead (crucified) to the world (Galatians 5:24-26).

Justification

Justification is an important aspect of salvation. It differs from regeneration in that, in regeneration, we see that man receives a new life and a new nature, whereas in justification God adds the fact that we have a new standing.

Justification is that act of God whereby He declares righteous the sinner who believes in Christ. It is a reversal of God's attitude toward a sinner, because of the sinner's new relation to Christ. God turns toward such a person.

To *justify* is "to reckon, to declare, or to show righteous" (like an identification photograph). To justify does not mean to make righteous. It is a legal term declaring a man to be in good standing. God's court differs from a human court of law in that, in God's court, all sins must be paid for and the sinner punished; there is no pardon without payment. In a human court, a person may be pardoned, a crime forgiven but not paid for. The Christian who is justified in God's court is not a pardoned criminal; he is a righteous man, declared to be so by God because of Christ's death.

To misunderstand justification is to fall into error. For instance, during medieval days the doctrine was subverted by the Roman Catholic teaching that it is a subjective experience, and that justification infuses new habits of grace. They mixed up sanctification and justification and thus interjected (human) works into salvation. The reformers came along and pointed out this error, though they neglected the aspects of regeneration and sanctification until the Wesleyan days.

Three things are incorporated into God's justification:

- Forgiveness—remission of the penalty. The penalty for sin is death (Genesis 2:16-17; Romans 5:12-14), spiritual, physical, and eternal. To be saved is to have this penalty removed (Isaiah 53:5, 6; 1 Peter 2:24). Since Christ has borne man's penalty for sin, God now remits that penalty for the believer (Romans 8:1, 33, 34; 2 Corinthians 5:21).

- Imputation of righteousness. This is the exchanging of accounts—an accountant term (Psalms 32:2). "Blessed is the man to whom the Lord imputeth not iniquity and in whose spirit there is no guile." "Until the law sin was in the world: but sin is not imputed when there is no law" (Romans 5:13). Sinners are not only pardoned for past sins, but also supplied with a positive righteousness, so that we can have fellowship with God (Romans 4:8: "Blessed is the man to whom the Lord will not impute sin"). Christ's righteousness came over to our account, our sins went to His account, and He paid for them by His death.

- Fellowship—restoration to favor. The sinner has both incurred a penalty and lost God's favor (John 3:36;

Romans 1:18, 5:9; Galatians 2:16, 17). The civil rights of a pardoned criminal may be restored, but often the criminal is not reconciled to society. In contrast with human law, we are restored to acceptance by God.

The Method of Justification

- Negatively:
  - Not by works (Romans 4:4, 5, 11:6).
  - Not by deeds of the law (Galatians 3:11, 3:20, 2:16).
- Positively:
  - By the grace of God (Romans 3:24; Titus 3:5, 7).
  - By the blood of Jesus (Romans 3:24, 5:9; Hebrews 9:22).
  - By faith (Romans 3:26-30, 5:1; Galatians 2:16).
  - By resurrection (Romans 4:24, 25).

The Results of Justification

- Remission of penalty (Romans 4:7, 8; 2 Corinthians 5:19; Romans 8:1, among others).
- Restoration to favor (Romans 4:6; 1 Corinthians 1:30; 2 Corinthians 5:21).
- Imputation of Christ's righteousness (Romans 4:5).
- Heirship (Titus 3:7).
- Direct result in practical living (Philippians 1:11; 1 John 3:7).
- Assurance that one is saved from the coming wrath of God (Romans 5:9; 1 Thessalonians 1:10).
- Assurance of coming glorification (Romans 8:30; Matthew 13:43; Galatians 5:5).

Sanctification

This aspect of salvation is very confused today, because of the great emphasis some place upon experience; some claim that sanctification and experience are one, or interpret the doctrine of sanctification on the basis of experience. Really, only one of three parts of sanctification deals with the problem of human experience. It is the function of the Bible to interpret experience—but we must be careful not to use experience to interpret the Bible. Every experience that is wrought of God will be found to be in accordance with Scripture.

Definition of Sanctification

Sanctification indicates being set apart; or the state of being set apart; or, Scripturally, "to be set apart from sin unto God." Sanctification deals with holiness, or "Christian perfection" (defined later in this chapter).

The words *sanctify, holy,* and *saint* come from the same Hebrew word (*godesh*) and Greek word (*hagiazo*). This is an important subject in the Bible. *Sanctify* in its various forms is used 106 times in the Old Testament and 31 times in the New Testament. *Holy* is used 400 times in the Old Testament and 12 times (referring to believers) in the New Testament. *Saint* is used of Israel 50 times and of the believers 62 times. The Holy Spirit describes believers as *brothers* 184 times, as *saints* 62 times, and as Christians only 3 times.

Hebrews 12:14 says, "Follow after peace with all men, and the sanctification without which no man shall see the Lord." This teaches us to be sanctified, to sanctify God, and to sanctify certain things unto Him. He expects this, and to resist it and neglect it is sin (1 Thessalonians 4:3, 7: "This is the will of God even your sanctification, that you should abstain from fornication . . . For God hath not called us into uncleanness but unto holiness").

Sanctification is not:

- Betterment of the flesh (1 Corinthians 2:9-16). It is not the work of the Holy Spirit to improve the old sin nature; that nature cannot understand the Holy Spirit. Christ was sanctified and so was the Sabbath.

- Eradication of the old sin nature (1 John 1). There are those who claim that a sanctified person is incapable of sinning. How about verses like 1 Corinthians 7:14? Is it possible for a wife to eradicate the sinful nature of an unsaved husband? How about carnal Christians who are sanctified (1 Corinthians 1:1, 2, 3:1, 3)?

☙ To be "holier than thou" or sanctimonious. A believer is not to be hypocritical, affected, or devout in a hypocritical way; Christ's greatest enemies were the Pharisees and religious leaders.

☙ A "second blessing" or a spiritual relationship gained after salvation that some achieve and others don't.

Sanctification is:

☙ To be set apart for a purpose. An unsaved man can sanctify unto sin (Isaiah 66:17), but the believer is sanctified unto God; he is separated unto God as a tabernacle (Exodus 40:10, 11; Numbers 7:1).

☙ To have imputation of Christ as our holiness (1 Corinthians 1:30, 1:2). All believers are saints irrespective of their spiritual attainments (Romans 1:7; 1 Corinthians 1:2; Ephesians 1:1).

Results of Sanctification

☙ Purification of moral evil should be a result of our positional sanctification (dealt with later):
  ☙ priests (Exodus 19:22).
  ☙ believers today (2 Corinthians 6:17, 18).
  ☙ from false teachers and doctrines (2 Timothy 2:12; 2 John 9, 10).

☙ Conformation to the image of Christ is a positive aspect of sanctification (Romans 8:29; Galatians 5:22, 23; Philippians 1:6; 1 John 3:2; others).

Three Aspects of Sanctification or the Time of Sanctification

☙ Positional sanctification—First aspect/initial act. The moment a person believes, that person is God's and is declared to be so. Such persons are called saints irrespective of spiritual attainments (1 Corinthians 1:2; Ephesians 1:1; Colossians 1:2; Hebrews 10:10; Jude 1, 3).

- Experiential sanctification—Second aspect. This is the process of sanctification that continues throughout the believer's life: As he walks in the Spirit, obedient to the Word, the believer "grows in grace and knowledge of our Lord and Saviour Jesus Christ" (2 Peter 3:18). Other evidences follow the initial surrender (Romans 6:13, 12:1):
  - "Put to death deeds of the body" (Romans 8:13).
  - "Work in him obedience to the Word" (1 Peter 1:22).
  - Produce "fruit of spirit" (Galatians 5:22, 23).
  - "Increase and abound in love" (1 Thessalonians 3:12).
  - "Perfect holiness in the fear of God" (2 Corinthians 7:1).
  - "Be transformed into the image of Christ" (2 Corinthians 3:18; Ephesians 4:11-15).

  This does not mean sinless perfection; Noah was called a saint but became shamefully drunk. Lot, too, is called righteous. Matthew 5:48 says, "Ye, therefore, shall be perfect, as your heavenly Father is perfect," which obviously refers to displaying love to both good and bad. If *saint* referred to human beings becoming like God, none would ever be called a saint.

- Complete sanctification—Third aspect. The completion of salvation will take place either at death (Hebrews 12:23) or at His coming (1 John 3:2; Hebrews 9:28; Jude 23; others).

The Means of Sanctification

- God is eternally sanctified because of infinite holiness.
- The Trinity is said to sanctify persons.
  - Father (1 Thessalonians 5:23).
  - Son (Ephesians 5:26; Hebrews 2:11, 9:12-14, 13:12).
  - Holy Spirit (Romans 15:16; 2 Thessalonians 2:13).
- God the Father sanctifies the Son (John 10:36).
- God sanctifies the priests and people of Israel (Exodus 29:44, 31:13).

- Our sanctification is the will of God (1 Thessalonians 4:3).
- Our sanctification from God is by:
  - Our union with Christ (1 Corinthians 1:2, 30).
  - The Word of God (John 17:17).
  - The blood of Christ (Hebrews 9:13, 13:12).
  - The body of Christ (Hebrews 10:10).
  - The Spirit (1 Peter 1:2).
  - Our own choice (Hebrews 12:14; 2 Timothy 2:21, 22).
  - Faith (Acts 26:18).
- God sanctifies days, places, things (Genesis 2:3; Exodus 29:43).
- Man may sanctify God (Matthew 6:9; 1 Peter 3:15: "hallowed be thy name").
- Man may sanctify self (2 Timothy 2:21; 2 Corinthians 6:17, 7:1).
- Man may sanctify persons and things (1 Corinthians 7:14; Exodus 19:14).

Adoption

The usual meaning of the word *adopt* is to place a person rightfully outside blood ties into the position of a legal child. Instances of this appear in Scripture, such as when Moses was adopted by Pharaoh's daughter (Exodus 2:10); Esther, too, was adopted in this sense (Esther 2:7, 15).

However, we find the word *adoption* used in a different manner, exclusively by Paul, in five passages: Romans 8:15, 23, 9:4; Galatians 4:5; and Ephesians 1:5. It is obvious that Paul considers this a facet of salvation, so our study here is to dig out this special emphasis of salvation.

Meaning of the Scriptural Word Huidthesia

The word *huidthesia,* used five times by Paul, means to be placed as a mature son (as in the Jewish *bar mitzvah* or Roman *toga virilis*).

As we read the Pauline passages on this subject, we conclude that there are four uses of the word, namely:

1. In reference to Israel as compared to the unbelieving gentiles in their own dispensation (Romans 9:4). They were considered by the Lord to be a member of the family by His sovereign choice.

2. Three aspects of adoption deal with the meaning to the believer in this dispensation.

    ❧ Past aspect (Romans 8:15-17) emphasizes our position, in that we are children of God who have already received the assurance of being treated by God as a full-fledged part of God's family; plan on being an heir with Christ. This is also emphasized in Galatians 4:5 and Ephesians 1:5 (accepted in the beloved).

    ❧ Present aspect (Romans 8:14-17; Galatians 4:1-14), where we are to live victoriously, under the power of the indwelling Spirit (Romans 8:16); not under the law as servants (Galatians 4:6-14), but rather as sons (*uios*, not *teknon*).

    ❧ Future aspect lies in the truth that our bodies shall someday be redeemed; this is emphasized in Romans 8:23.

3. Another phase is dispensational. In Galatians 3:9 to 4:11, *adoption* refers to the fact the Jews, under law, were servants but we, under grace, are to be sons. Luke 15:25-32 refers to the elder son who worked in the field as a servant (Luke 15:25), and knew less than the servants (15:26), whereas, as the son referred to in verse 31, he heard, "Son thou art ever with me—all of mine is thine."

4. Another phase is maturity in the believer's life. As we study Romans 8:14-17, we note the interchange of the Greek words *uios* (sons) and *teknon* (children). The *uios* of verse 14 refers to those led of the Spirit as mature sons, whereas *teknon* is used throughout the rest of the passage to refer to blessings received by every believer, whether mature or not.

Also, Galatians 4:1-9 refers to immature children being under law, whereas a son enjoys freedom from bondage.

Redemption (Romans 3:24)

The facets of salvation we have studied so far have been the beauty of regeneration, the status of justification, the power of sanctification, and the responsibility of adoption. Now we look at the freedom of redemption.

The Bible is full of redemption. It is God's character to save and that's what Christ's mission to earth was. *To redeem the lost.* This is the whole message of the Word, and to fail to emphasize this is to ignore the whole reason for our existence.

Redemption refers to slavery; more specifically, it means a transaction in which a slave is purchased from slavery and set free to choose whether to serve the redeemer who purchased the slave. The word is presented in three ways:

1. To buy in a slave market.

2. To purchase out of a market.

3. To loose or set free.

We study Old Testament and New Testament references to redemption. Also, look at the *New Scofield Bible*'s note on Isaiah 59:20.

Old Testament References to Redemption

✶ Israel redeemed as a nation out of Egypt (Exodus 6:6; Isaiah 63:4).

✶ One animal redeemed by another (Exodus 13:13).

✶ A lost estate redeemed by kinsman (Leviticus 25:25, 49); this is the type of Christ's redemption.

    ↝ A redeemer must be a near kinsman.

    ↝ He must have the price of redemption; ability to pay.

    ↝ He must be willing to redeem (Hebrews 10:4-10).

    ↝ He must be qualified to redeem and not a slave himself.

New Testament References to Redemption

- ➴ We are all slaves sold under sin (Romans 7:14; 1 Corinthians 12:2; Ephesians 2:2) and condemned to die (John 3:18; Romans 3:19; Galatians 3:10).

- ➴ The price for redemption from sin is blood (Hebrews 9:27, 28: "And it is appointed unto man…").

- ➴ No return to former slavery—redeemer will not sell a slave he bought (John 10:28).

- ➴ Emancipation (John 8:36; Romans 8:19-21; Galatians 4:31; 5:13).

ASSURANCE

Though the terms *redemption* and *assurance* are used interchangeably by some, they really emphasize two different aspects of salvation. As we continue our study of salvation, we now emphasize the blessing of these two parts of our salvation.

Assurance is a confidence that right relations exist between one's self and God. In extreme cases of lack of assurance, some feel that they never had, or have lost, their salvation. God wants the believer to have assurance—to know that he or she is saved and resting in God (Hebrews 10:22: "Let us draw near with a true heart in full assurance of faith"; Hebrews 6:11: "to the full assurance of hope unto the end"; 2 Timothy 1:12: "I know whom I have believed"; Colossians 2:2: "Unto all riches of the full assurance of understanding").

Two Proofs of Salvation or Reasons for Assurance

CHRISTIAN EXPERIENCE:

- ➴ Inward witness of the Spirit (Romans 8:16; 1 John 5:9, 10).

- ➴ The difference between "children of God" and "children of the devil"—the latter practices sin without confession and repentance.

- ❧ The believer cannot sin without inner distress (Psalms 32:3-5; 1 John 1:8, 10).

- ❧ A believer examines and proves himself or herself (2 Corinthians 13:5).

- ❧ Some positive experiences verify our relationship with God, such as:
  - ❧ The Word of God is desired.
  - ❧ A passion for the salvation of man.
  - ❧ The Fatherhood of God becomes a personal belief (Matthew 11:27, 28).
  - ❧ Prayer becomes a reality.
  - ❧ A kinship exists (1 John 3:14).

THE WORD OF GOD PROVES OUR RELATIONSHIP:

- ❧ 1 John 5:13: "That ye may know that ye have eternal life."

- ❧ 2 Timothy 1:12: "I know whom I have believed."

- ❧ John 6:37: "Him that cometh to me I will in no wise cast out."

Two Reasons for Doubting Salvation

- ❧ One doubts his own committal—obvious cure is to receive Christ now.

- ❧ Doubting faithfulness of God. This is usually the result of a lack of Bible study and basing one's beliefs about salvation on feelings. Cure is to study the Word to find out the attributes of God and recognize anew that our salvation depends on Christ's work, not our own.

Eternal Security of the Believer

Volumes have been written on this subject, both pro and con, depending on upon whether the author takes an Armenian or a Calvinistic viewpoint. We can only touch upon the many reasons why we believe that a true believer can never be lost. This position is entirely harmonious with the gospel of grace. To hold that men can lose their salvation some time after being saved interjects man's efforts and righteousness into the picture at some juncture, which is error. Following are reasons and Scriptural passages that teach the eternal security of the believer.

BECAUSE OF THE MINISTRY OF THE HOLY SPIRIT, WHICH:

- Regenerates (2 Corinthians 5:17; Ephesians 2:10; Galatians 6:15; John 3:7).
- Indwells forever (abides) (John 14:16, 17; 1 John 2:27).
- Baptizes (Acts 1:5).
- Seals (2 Corinthians 1:21, 22; Ephesians 1:13, 14, 4:30; Romans 8:23).

BECAUSE OF THE MINISTRY OF CHRIST:

- His death, not my righteousness or works, pays for sin (1 John 2:2); the believer must be condemned either for every sin or for none.
- His resurrection.
  - The believer is raised in Christ; terms "eternal life" and "shall not perish" in Colossians 2, 3; Ephesians 2:1.
  - The believer is part of the new creation over which Christ is the head.
- Christ advocates (1 John 1:1–2:2).
- Christ intercedes (John 17:1-26; Romans 8:34; Luke 22:31-34; Hebrews 7:23-25).

BECAUSE OF GOD:

- His sovereign purpose (Ephesians 1:11, 12; Romans 8:28-30). God is interested in means, we in ends.
- His power (John 10:28, 29; Romans 4:21, 8:31, 38, 39, 14:4).
- The infinite love of God (Romans 5:8, 9, 10; Colossians 1:27; John 3:16).
- God's love that brings forth the will of God concerning His relationship to His divine family (Hebrews 12:3-15).

OTHER SCRIPTURAL FACTS THAT CONFIRM
THE SECURITY OF THE BELIEVER:

- Our salvation was accomplished by Christ, not by us or any men. Christ's work is perfect and complete.

- Man's works never save and do not enter into the keeping of salvation. Salvation is only by Christ's blood.

- The direct promises of God, such as in John 10:28, 29; Philippians 1:6; and Romans 8:28-39. Also, the words "eternal" and "shall not perish" in Psalms 23:1, 91:1, etc.

- The fact that there is provision for confession and forgiveness.

- Truth of carnal Christians vs. spiritual Christians.

- Fact that Christ is our advocate and stands before God for us.

- Family terms used in Scripture to describe believers; illustrated by the prodigal son. We're sons and heirs.

- Scriptural illustration of David, Samson, Jacob, Lot (2 Samuel 11, 12; Psalms 38–40).

- The divine nature within us.

- The fact that we have been delivered from the law.

- The execution of divine purpose.
  - Issue is advocacy (1 John 1, 2).
  - Three sides of one parable (Luke 15). Issue is how to restore lost sheep—not goats!

Eternal Security of the Believer: Verses and Reasons Compiled from Class Involvement

- Can a true believer perish? Christ says never—"I give unto them eternal life and they shall never perish" (John 10:28, 3:15, 16, 6:39).

- We are told that "he who doeth the will of My Father shall enter into the kingdom of heaven" (Matthew 7:21). This is substantiated in John 6:40. Repentance of David and assurance of seeing his son (2 Samuel 12:23; 1 John 1:9). As believers, we are to rejoice because our names are written in heaven—the Lamb's book of life (Luke 10:20; Revelation 21:27, 22:5).

✤ We read, "Neither is there salvation in any other; for there is no other name under heaven given among men, whereby we must be saved" (Acts 4:12). That we must be saved implies that someone else must do the saving. We can't save ourselves, because we all are sinners and fall short of the glory of God. Thus, we cannot begin by standing on the merits of Christ and end by standing on our own. One cannot be saved (eternal life) by grace and retain or lose it through merit, works, actions, or deeds (Ephesians 2:8, 9; Romans 10:13; Revelation 22:17; John 6:37).

✤ As believers we are joint-heirs with Christ, and our inheritance is incorruptible and undefiled; it fadeth not away, but is reserved in heaven for us (1 Peter 1:4, 5; 1 John 2:17; 2 Corinthians 5:1; Philippians 3:20, 21).

✤ When one believes and trusts in the finished work of Christ, his salvation is secure. There can be no progress or change in the believer's security, for there is no progress in a work already finished (John 19:30).

✤ The "righteous" shall inherit "eternal life" and the only righteousness we have is imputed to us by God through Christ Jesus (Philippians 3:9; Romans 1:17, 3:22). When this righteousness is imputed by God to the believer, it becomes his (the believer's) forever (John 14:16).

✤ The Good Shepherd has pledged His holy Word that no sheep of His shall ever perish. It is the *unbeliever* who is not His sheep (John 10:26). Why not honor His blessed Word and take the comfort for your soul that such an assurance affords?

✤ The Bible teaches us everything under the heading "Christ's work as priest," including His present intercession for us. He saved us completely and forever. The Christian could be lost again only if Christ failed as a priest, which he could not and did not do. He will always be with us and His love will never end. His Word will always be a source of inspiration and guidance.

There are also these verses, which were submitted by numerous members of the class (uncensored and unabridged). Please read and think about each verse.

Psalms 31:23
Malachi 3:6
Matthew 7:21-23
John 1:12; 3:14-18; 3:36; 5:24; 6:37, 39, 44, 47; 10:27-29;
     14:16, 19; 15:16; 17:2, 3
Acts 4:12; 13:48
Romans 1:16; 3:24; 8:15, 16, 26-39; 10:4, 9-13
1 Corinthians 5:8
Galatians 3:22
Ephesians 1:4
Philippians 1:3-7, 12-14, 23; 3:20; 4:30
Colossians 3:13
1 Thessalonians 4:17
1 Timothy 6:12
2 Timothy 4:7, 8; 2:13, 19
Titus 1:2; 3:7
Hebrews 1:14; 5:9; 6:4-6; 7:24, 25; 9:12, 15;
     10:14, 22-26; 13:5
1 Peter 1:3-5; 4:19
2 Peter 3:13
1 John 1:1, 2, 9; 2:19, 25; 3:14, 19; 4:13; 5:10-14, 20
Revelation 14:13

ELECTION

The doctrine of election is a cardinal teaching of Scripture. It does present many problems to the finite mind; however, we must remember that the Word of God is not to be altered or any part of its teaching neglected. God does not need human beings to censor His Word or to decide the importance or acceptability of His teachings.

We must remember that revelation and not reason is the guide to faith. When God speaks, we are just to listen and acquiesce. God is honored by believing and resting in Him.

Election refers to the fact that the favor of God—notably a free salvation—is accorded to some but not to all; the recipients are chosen in God's sovereign wisdom (and there are many illustrations of God's sovereign wisdom). There are many existing illustrations of God's election, such as men being born not of the same race, same advantages, or same native abilities. Some natural things show forth more glory than others: for example, some live longer and have more opportunities than others.

Problems with election are numerous, and we will deal with them in greater detail later in this section. The primary problem, though, is the reconciliation of divine election with the universality of divine love. Let's study the Scriptural presentation of this doctrine and endeavor to see the necessity of understanding its implications and accepting its truth.

Scriptural Terms Synonymous with Election

In Scripture, the elect are referred to as: chosen, called, "My sheep," etc. Election is also termed foreknowledge, predestination, drawing, divine purpose, foreordained, appointed, etc.

Scriptural Passages

Some Scriptural passages declare the fact of election, for both Israel and the believer:

Isaiah 46:9, 10
Mark 13:20, 22, 27
Luke 18:7
John 15:16, 19; 17:8, 9
Acts 13:48
Romans 8:29; 9:11-13, 22, 23; 11:5, 7; 16:13
Ephesians 1:4, 5
Colossians 1:26-29
1 Thessalonians 5:9

2 Thessalonians 2:13, 14
2 Timothy 1:9
1 Peter 1:2

There are also examples of choice, such as Elijah's widow in Zarepath, Naaman the leper, Mary, the apostles, Saul, Jacob over Esau, and so on.

Problems Posed by Some to the Doctrine of Election

๙ The solemn problem of retribution, or the fact that God has rejected some, as evidenced by verses such as Revelation 13:8; Romans 9:22; Jude 1:4; 1 Peter 2:8; Malachi 1:2, 3; Romans 9-11. It is plain that these persons are guilty, but some say that their evil does not deserve eternal separation from God.

๙ The main disagreement between Calvinists and Armenians centers on predestination and free will. Objections to election revolve around (1) the moral character of God and (2) the moral agency of man. The latter has been dealt with, but listed below are objections relating to the former:

  ๛ Justice of God questioned; God is put forth as a respecter of persons. *Answer:* God saves some only on basis of grace—no human merit ever enters in.

  ๛ Love of God—He couldn't send anyone to hell. *Answer:* For greater reasons, unrevealed to man, God does not gratify all His desires, nor has He revealed them to us.

  ๛ Predestination predetermines that man shall sin. *Answer:* This is totally inconsistent with Scripture (Romans 6:1-10).

  ๛ Predestination discourages free will. *Answer:* Election includes everything necessary to accomplish the end, including call, justification, glorification, etc.

  ๛ God is unjust to those not included in salvation. *Answer:* To the contrary! He should be praised for saving *anyone.*

  ๛ God is arbitrary. *Answer:* He has free choice to exercise sovereignty in His wisdom, which is inscrutable to us.

- Election tends to promote immorality by giving salvation to a man even if he doesn't care. *Answer:* No! Sanctification answers this.
- It inspires pride for the elect. *Answer:* To the contrary! If properly taught and understood, election should inspire humility.
- It discourages the giving out of the message, because man's destiny is determined (fatalism). *Answer:* A call must go to the elect, and no man knows who is elect and who isn't. It is a secret decree. God has ordained that we should be the messengers of the message in the Great Commission. Man is still urged to choose and is responsible to do so if he is saved; to reject is to confirm that he is of the nonelect.

Truths of Divine Election

- God, by election, has chosen some to salvation but not all (dealt with above).

- Election was accomplished in eternity past (Ephesians 1:4; 2 Timothy 1:9; Acts 15:18; 2 Thessalonians 2:13, 14: "From the beginning").

- Election does not merely rest in foreknowledge; 1 Peter 1:2 deals with the order in contrast to Romans 8:29, but Acts 2:23 tells of God's plan. Important: we are saved by grace, not by our inclinations or works or leanings toward salvation (Romans 11:5, 6).

- Election is immutable. God is not dependent on the whims of men, and God doesn't adjust Himself to the will of men (2 Timothy 2:18, 19; Romans 8:30).

Positive Thoughts about the Doctrine of Election

I do not have to vindicate my Master and prove His justice. He speaks for Himself—but this we do know:

- He has saved everyone who comes to Him; therefore, they are elected.

- Those who don't desire to be saved, He doesn't force—therefore, they are not elected.

- If a man prefers sin, drunkenness, and the world to becoming a holy son of God, why should he grumble when God elects one who wishes to be a son and live a holy life?

- Also, if a man chooses to live in sin, why do we call God unjust if God does not force that man, by election, to come to Himself? Why should the unsaved man care if God gives something to another that the unbeliever does not want? If He saves one man who desires to be saved, and if I don't want to be saved, why should I care if I don't get saved?

- For the Christian:
  - Election causes us to be humble when we see that we are saved totally and only by grace. Salvation did not depend on what we are or were, and we are not chosen on the basis of works or personality (after all, God even gives us original faith). Every virtue comes from Him and God doesn't save on the basis of foreknowledge. Election is absolute and altogether apart from the virtues that saints have afterward. Before He saves men, they are hopeless.
  - Election is personal—God saved me, for His purpose.
  - Elect people are holy, distinct, marked from others—marks are holiness, separation, and faith; we're to walk believing that we are chosen of God. James tells us that our lives will show that we are elect (1 Peter 1:1, 2; Colossians 1:26-29).
  - Election should make me bold, because I know I am God's and saved to serve Him.

THE RICHES OF DIVINE GRACE

Blessings we have in Christ (as compiled by Chafer, 1948, vol. 3, pp. 234–65):

- In the eternal plan of God: Foreknow (1 Peter 1:2, 20); predestined (Romans 8:29); elect of God (1 Thessalonians 1:4); chosen (Ephesians 1:4); called (Hebrews 1:14).

- Redeemed—three aspects (Romans 3:24, 8:23; Ephesians 1:7).

- Reconciled (2 Corinthians 5:20).

- Related to God through propitiation—turning away of wrath by an offering (1 John 2:2).

- Forgiven all trespasses (Colossians 2:13).

- Vitally conjoined to Christ for the Judgment of the Old Man "unto a new walk" (Romans 6:1-10).

- Free from the law (John 1:17; Acts 15:24-29; Romans 6:14, 7:2-6).

- Children of God (John 1:12, 3:6; 1 Peter 1:23).

- Adopted (Ephesians 1:4, 5).

- Acceptable to God by Jesus Christ (Ephesians 1:6; 1 Peter 2:5).
  - Made righteous (2 Corinthians 5:21).
  - Sanctified positionally (1 Corinthians 6:11; Ephesians 5:27; 1 John 3:2).
  - Perfected forever (Hebrews 10:14).
  - Made accepted in the beloved (Ephesians 1:6).
  - Made meet—fit for service and celestial glory (Colossians 1:12).

- Justified (Romans 3:24, 4:5).

- Made nigh (Ephesians 2:13, James 4:8).

- Delivered from the power of darkness (Colossians 1:13).

- Translated into the Kingdom of the Son of His love (Colossians 1:13).

- On the Rock, Jesus Christ (Matthew 7:24-27).

- A gift from God the Father to Christ (John 17:2, 6, 9, 11, 12, 24).

- Circumcised in Christ (Ephesians 2:11; Colossians 2:11).

- Partakers of the holy and royal priesthood (1 Peter 2:5-9; Revelation 1:6).

- A chosen generation, a holy nation, a peculiar people (1 Peter 2:9).

- Heavenly citizens (Philippians 3:20; Luke 10:20; Hebrews 11:10, 40).

- Of the family and household of God (Ephesians 2:19; Galatians 6:10).

- In the fellowship of the saints (John 17:11, 21-23).

- A heavenly association:
  - Partners with Christ in life (Colossians 1:27; 1 John 5:11, 12).
  - Partnership in position (Colossians 3:1).
  - Partners with Christ in service (1 Corinthians 1:9).
  - Partners with Christ in suffering (2 Timothy 2:12; 1 Peter 4:12, 13).
  - Partners with Christ in prayer (John 14:12-14).
  - Partners with Christ in betrothal (2 Corinthians 11:2).
  - Partners in expectation (Titus 2:13).

- Having access to God:
  - Access into His grace (Romans 5:2).
  - Access unto the Father (1 Corinthians 2:10, 12:13; 2 Corinthians 3:14).
  - Access is reassuring (Hebrews 4:16, 10:19, 20).

- Within the care of God (Romans 5:8-10).
  - Objects of His love (John 3:16; Romans 5:8; 1 John 3:16).
  - Objects of His grace:
    - Salvation (Ephesians 2:7-9).
    - Safekeeping (Romans 5:2).
    - Service (John 17:18; Ephesians 4:7).
    - Instruction (Titus 2:12, 13).
  - Objects of His power (Ephesians 1:19; Philippians 2:13).
  - Objects of His faithfulness (Hebrews 13:5; Philippians 1:6).
  - Objects of His peace (Romans 5:1).
  - Objects of His consolation (2 Thessalonians 2:16, 17).
  - Objects of His intercession (Romans 8:26; Ephesians 6:18; Jude 1:20).

- His inheritance (Ephesians 1:18; John 17:22).

- The inheritance of the saints (1 Peter 1:4).

- Light in the Lord (1 John 1:5; 2 Corinthians 4:6).

- Vitally united with the Father, Son, and Holy Spirit (1 Thessalonians 1:1; Ephesians 4:6; Romans 8:1, 9; John 14:20; 1 Corinthians 2:12).

- Blessed with earnest or first-fruits of Spirit (2 Corinthians 1:22; Ephesians 1:14; Romans 8:23).

- Glorified (Romans 8:18; Colossians 3:4).

- Complete in Him (Colossians 2:9, 10).

- Possessing every spiritual blessing (Ephesians 1:3).

Ecclesiology

Doctrine of the Church

∽∾

INTRODUCTION

The word *ecclesia* is often translated in the New Testament as "church"; however, it really means "a called-out company" or "assembly." Though we will be looking at references that are translated as "church," we must also acknowledge that, on the basis of context, the word was translated as "mob" in Acts 19:30-32, 35, 39, and 41, and as "assembly" (Israel was termed an assembly but not the church in Acts 7:38).

We will study the obvious references to the "called-out company" or "assembly," from the world to Christ, in this doctrinal study. Our outline for study is:

What is the church?
> Three major divisions; definition
> A New Testament revelation—mystery
> Membership
> Christ's relationship to the church
> Purpose

The church's commission, service, stewardship, and worship

What the church is not

The local church
> Organization
> Ordinances
> Discipline
> Reward

I. What Is the Church?

Divisions of the Church

Three main divisions of the human race are the Jew, the gentile, and the church of God (1 Corinthians 10:32). We must understand these divisions to understand God's present purpose.

1. Jews are the nation that came from Abraham. According to divine purpose and promise, they are the chosen, earthly people of God. They've been miraculously preserved and will yet be the dominant, glorified people of the earth during the coming Kingdom age (Isaiah 62:1-11). Four words describe the working of the divine purpose in this people: "chosen," "scattered," "gathered," and "blessed." Note Romans 9:4, 5; Genesis 12:3.

2. Gentiles are all others who are not Jews. The blessings they receive are only in conjunction with the church of God in this present age and with the Jews during the Kingdom age.

3. *The church* refers to the whole company of the redeemed, both gentile and Jew, who will have been saved during the present age. Privileges accorded them are many, including:

   ❧ Entrance into the kingdom of God (John 3:5).

   ❧ Destined to be conformed to the image of Christ (Romans 8:29).

   ❧ In Christ, enjoying new-life status, promises, and hopes.

   ❧ Citizens of heaven (Philippians 3:20; Colossians 3:3); thus go to and are involved in heavenly interests.

A New Testament Revelation

The church is a mystery (Ephesians 3:3-6, 9), which means that the Old Testament did not prophesy about it or anticipate it in teachings. Many types illustrate it, but these were not seen by Old Testament believers. The church was first revealed to the apostle Paul.

Membership

The church is formed of both Jews and gentiles (Romans 3:9). The Jews did not understand that their covenants were set aside temporarily, as described in the book of Acts. The Jewish nation is blinded only during this age (Romans 11:25); after this age the Jew will respond to the Deliverer who will come out of Zion and enter into the time when all covenants between God and the Jews will be fulfilled. Paul was set apart by God to introduce this message. He had at least two revelations: one concerning the gospel of the grace of God (Galatians 1:11, 12), and the other concerning the church which is the body of Christ (Ephesians 3:3-6). The body is now one (Ephesians 2:15).

Membership in the invisible church comes automatically when one becomes a believer, for part of salvation is to be united with Christ through baptism by the Holy Spirit (1 Corinthians 12:13). The local church or visible church should be composed of believers only; it is natural for a believer to choose the fellowship of other saints. It is possible for one to be a member of the visible church but not the invisible; however, it is impossible to be a member of the invisible church without being saved and no longer of this world (John 17:16).

Christ's Sevenfold Relationship to the Church

1. Shepherd and His sheep (John 10):
   - Christ came by door; that is, through appointed lineage of David.
   - He is true Shepherd who is followed by true sheep.
   - Door of the sheep—entrance into salvation as well as door that provides security (John 10:28, 29).
   - Life and food are provided for the sheep by the Shepherd.
   - In contrast, other shepherds are merely hirelings.
   - There is fellowship between sheep and shepherd as Father knows Son.

⊰ In present age, one fold for both Jew and gentile (John 10:16).

⊰ As Shepherd, Christ ever lives to intercede for the sheep, but also lays down His life for His sheep.

2. Vine and branches (John 15). Christ is true vine and believers are branches (John 15). Central truth is that there is no joy or fruit apart from vine. Results of abiding are:

⊰ Cleansing and pruning (15:2).

⊰ Effectual prayer (15:7).

⊰ Celestial joy (15:11).

⊰ Eternal truth (15:16).

3. Cornerstone and building (Ephesians 2:19-22). Building built on foundation (cornerstone) of Christ and apostles (Ephesians 2:19-22; 1 Peter 2:5). Abides in us.

⊰ Old Testament Jew had temple; now church is temple.

⊰ Christ is chief cornerstone and individual believers are stones of building (Ephesians 2:19-22).

⊰ It is God's present purpose to build His church (Matthew 16:18).

⊰ Each stone is a living stone because it partakes of the divine nature (1 Peter 2:5); Christ is chief cornerstone and foundation (1 Corinthians 3:11; Ephesians 2:20-22; 1 Peter 2:6) and the building as a whole becomes a habitation of God through the Spirit (Ephesians 2:22).

4. Our High Priest over believer priests. Believer priest has a four-fold sacrifice:

⊰ Offers a service of sacrifice, presenting himself once and for all to God (Romans 12:1, 2).

⊰ Offers a service of worship in giving praise and thanksgiving to God (Hebrews 13:15), including a service of intercession on behalf of his own need and others (Romans 8:26, 27; Colossians 4:12; 1 Timothy 2:1; Hebrews 10:19-22).

٭ Offers sacrifice of good works.

٭ Offers sacrifice of his substance in addition to offering his body as a living sacrifice (Hebrews 13:16).

5. As head and body (1 Corinthians 12:12-14, 25-27); an organism composed of many members, with Christ as the head and the church as the body. Church as body has four characteristics:

٭ Oneness: complete, whole, unified.

٭ Deathlessness: it will never die.

٭ Manifestation: purpose of body is to reveal Christ, our head (Philippians 1:21) and the present purpose of God.

٭ Service: plans of Head are to be carried out by body.

The body is:

٭ Self-developing (Ephesians 4:11-16).

٭ Appointed to specific service, according to gifts given to us by God.

٭ Living organism united eternally in Christ.

6. Last Adam and new creation: A figure of Christ the resurrected one replacing Adam and the old order; church as the new creation.

7. Bridegroom and bride: A picture of future relationship between church and Christ in which church is the bride (Revelation 22:17; Ephesians 5:25-32):

٭ Who is purchased by Christ (Ephesians 5:25).

٭ Who is espoused to Christ (2 Corinthians 11:2); waiting for marriage.

٭ Who will be married to Christ (Revelation 19:7, 8; Matthew 25:1).

This in contrast with Israel, who was unfaithful wife to Jehovah. This is the only figure that has prophetic significance (2 Corinthians 11:2; Ephesians 5:25-33). In Ephesians 5 we see threefold work of Christ.

٭ Christ loved church and gave Himself for it (5:25).

- Christ is engaged in present work that He might sanctify and cleanse church (5:26).

- That He might present to Himself a glorious church not having spot or wrinkle (5:27).

We also see five characteristics of divine love for His church (Chafer, vol. 4, 1948).

- Eternal duration, because God is love (1 John 4:8).

- Motivation for ceaseless activity (Romans 5:8; 1 John 3:16).

- Transparent purity—He receives nothing, bestows everything (1 Peter 1:22).

- Limitless intensity (Romans 5:8-10, 39).

- Inexhaustible benevolence (John 15:13; Romans 3:2; Ephesians 2:8, 4; Titus 3:4, 5).

Purpose of the Church

The New Testament reveals that the church is the central purpose of God in the present age. It is a company of believers, formed of both Jew and gentile, who are called out of the world and joined together in one loving union by the baptism of the Holy Spirit (1 Corinthians 12:13; John 17:6-18).

Its present divine purpose in the world is not to convert the world, but rather a calling-out from the world of those who will believe in Christ to form the body of Christ. The world will be converted following rather than preceding the return of Christ: "We are not appointed of God to a world improvement program but to be a witness in all the world to Christ and of His saving grace and through this ministry of the Gospel preaching the spirit of God will accomplish the supreme divine purpose of this age" (Chafer, vol. 4, 1948).

Israel's covenants are yet to be fulfilled (Romans 11:27).

Three major characteristics of this age are described in Matthew 13:

- Israel's place in the world would be as a treasure hid in the field (Matthew 13:44).

- Evil continues to the end of this age (Matthew 13:4, 25, 33, 48; 2 Thessalonians 2:7).

- The children of this age shall be gathered out (Matthew 13:30, 45, 46, 48: likens them to wheat, to a pearl, to good fish). This shows God's supreme purpose in this age (Acts 15:13-19).

II. THE CHURCH'S COMMISSION, SERVICE, STEWARDSHIP, AND WORSHIP

Commission

We believers are commissioned of the Lord to be instant in season and out of season in an effort to win the lost (Mark 16:15; 2 Corinthians 5:19, 20). This ministry may be exercised in numerous ways (Chafer, vol. 4, 1948):

- Gospel may be presented to unsaved as a result of sacrificial gifts (Philippians 4:17, 18).

- Gospel may be presented in answer to prayer (John 14:14: "Ask anything in my name").

- Gospel may be presented by word of mouth of a Spirit-filled believer (Acts 1:8; 4:20).

- Gospel may be presented through indirect ministries such as radio, literature, music, educational institutions, etc.

Service

Service includes any work performed for the benefit of another.

God-appointed service is committed primarily to a divinely fitted priesthood (Leviticus; 1 Peter 2:5-9; Revelation 1:6). The Old Testament describes the divinely appointed ritual of the tabernacle and temple; New Testament is broader than Old Testament and is the anti-type of the Old Testament priesthood. New Testament priest is uniquely qualified by:

- Being cleansed at moment of salvation (Colossians 2:13; Titus 3:5: "Not by works ... by the washing of regeneration and renewing of the Holy Spirit").

❧ Being set apart by new birth into the family of God.

❧ Willingly dedicating himself to God (Romans 12:1, 2); "mercies of God" refer to salvation (Ephesians 2:10), not consecration, which is God's divine act of accepting and placing.

Priestly service involves:

❧ Dedication of self (Romans 12:1).

❧ Sacrifice of lips (Hebrews 13:15).

❧ Sacrifice of substance (Philemon 4:18).

❧ Sacrifice of good works (Hebrews 13:16).

❧ Worship (Hebrews 13:15).

❧ Service of intercession (Romans 8:26, 27; Hebrews 10:19-22; 1 Timothy 2:1; Colossians 4:12).

❧ Service toward men—gifts of service from God the indwelling Spirit (Romans 12:1-8; 1 Corinthians 12:8-11; Ephesians 4:11).

Two Old Testament prohibitions typify New Testament priestly attitudes:

❧ No strange incense (Exodus 30:9)—mere formality in service.

❧ No strange fire (Leviticus 10:1)—substitution of fleshly emotions in place of true devotion to the Word (e.g., Nadab and Abihu).

Stewardship

Three phases of stewardship:

1. Earning of money must be done in manner that glorifies God (1 Corinthians 10:31). We must all work (Genesis 3:19; 2 Thessalonians 3:10), but honorably.

2. Possession of money is a great responsibility for every believer. We must be careful to hold property only as God directs and dispense it according to His guiding.

3. Giving of money is an important part of a believer's service for God.

   ↦ A believer must first give himself (2 Corinthians 8:5), which, of course, means time, life, strength, abilities, etc.

   ↦ A believer must recognize God's authority over all that he has.

   ↦ Tithing is not imposed on the believer in this dispensation, but rather a grace giving (2 Corinthians 9:7).

Principles of New Testament giving (2 Corinthians 8–9):

↦ Christ was pattern (8:9).

↦ Even out of great poverty (8:2).

↦ Out of grace and love, not by commandment (9:7).

↦ First give oneself (8:5).

↦ Give systematically (1 Corinthians 16:2).

↦ God sustains giver (2 Corinthians 9:8-10; Luke 6:38).

↦ True riches are from God (2 Corinthians 8:9; Ephesians 1:7, 3:16).

Worship

Worship means prayer and thanksgiving (John 4:24). It is the adoration of the Christian heart. There are five aspects of prayer:

1. Praise and thanksgiving (Psalms 92, 98, 100, 104).

2. Presenting our own needs (John 14:13, 14).

3. Prayer in name of Christ (John 16:24; James 4:2, 3); when believer is no longer concerned with self, he prays right (2 Corinthians 5:17, 18; Colossians 3:3).

4. Wide scope, but with certain reasonable limitations:

   ↦ Heart conformed to mind of Christ (John 15:7; James 4:2, 3).

   ↦ Desire to do Christ's will (Philippians 2:13).

ɔ Spirit-filled (Romans 8:26, 27), which means no
unconfessed sin (1 John 1).

5. Prayer should be enjoyed by every believer regularly,
without vain repetitions.

III. What the Church Is Not

ɔ It is not Israel or spiritual Israel, as some say (Galatians 3:27-
29; 1 Corinthians 10:32; Ephesians 2:14, 15). Three confusing
passages are: John 1:47 (Nathaniel was a good Jew); Romans
2:28, 29 (referring to a true Jew); Galatians 6:15, 16 (refers to
believing and unbelieving Jew).

ɔ It is not the kingdom (church is called a temple in Ephesians
2:21; kingdom is never called a temple). Church is never the
subject of prophecy, whereas the kingdom is; church is to be
built up (Ephesians 4:12); kingdom is set up (Acts 15:16, etc.).

IV. The Local Church

Organization

A simple definition of the local church could be: an assembly of
professed believers meeting together in one locality. The church
started at Pentecost and became an ever-increasing, invisible,
divine force upon the earth. The consequence of this ever-
increasing bride of Christ is that it should manifest itself visible to
the world because of the evident change that was coming into
many lives. Thus local, visible churches were born, and as we look
into Scripture we see that this was God's plan for manifesting
Himself in this present church age—that is, through local
churches. Note Hebrews 10:25 as well as 1 Corinthians 16:19;
Acts 8:1; Romans 16:1; 1 Thessalonians 1:1, and many other
references to local churches (more than forty).

The progress of the local church proceeds from the New
Testament descriptions of it to a church in the fourth century that
seems to appropriate the Old Testament idea of a conquered world
under the rulership of a Messiah. The officials dreamed of a state

governed by the church even as Roman Catholics and Council of Churches do today; theirs was a postmillennial eschatology. The deterioration of the world and failure of the church to gain such power eventually led to changes such as the Reformation, when the church began to teach that Christ died only for the elect. The pendulum had swung. So often man's failure to establish a strong, spiritual, effective visible church lies in the fact that they were trying to build a lifeless organization rather than becoming a living organism, through whom Christ lived, led, and blessed. It's the same old story of a living, vital, grace-oriented approach in contrast to a dead, legalistic, manmade organization.

Some believe that because we see the church as a living organism, there should be no organization. Let's see the balance of Scripture, which advocates an organized group of Spirit-led people eager to please their Savior and Lord. We are sure that God intended church organization, because gifts and officers are named and duties defined.

Gifts given to the church are described in Ephesians 4:7, 8, 11:

- Apostles—first gift for apostolic days only.

- Prophets—to reach and teach by revelation until the canon (New Testament) was provided by God for church.

- Evangelists—men who fervently herald the Gospel. Still valid for today; pastor and all believers are also to evangelize (2 Timothy 4:5).

- Pastors and teachers—some are one or the other, and some are both. Pastor is shepherd of sheep and should also teach. Not all teachers are pastors, but all pastors should be teachers.

Officers are to provide leadership within the local church, as described in the New Testament. Officers include:

- Bishops, elders, and presbyters. All these hold the same office, but each name describes a different function. *Elder* was an older, mature leader who had proven himself. *Bishop* was an overseer (a functional position); *presbyter* was the speaking, teaching elder. All New Testament churches seem to have plural elders who had certain responsibilities, such as ruling the church (2 Timothy 3:4, 5, 5:17); watching for heresy (Titus 1:9); and superintending or overseeing the church as shepherds (John 21:16; Acts 20:28; Hebrews 13:17; 1 Peter 5:2). The number of elders undoubtedly depended on church size and how God gifted that church (Acts 14:23, 20:28; Titus 1:5; 1 Peter 5:2). A pastor, of course, is an elder (1 Timothy 3:1-7).

✎ Deacons (Acts 6:1-6; 1 Timothy 3:8-13) were set aside, in the early church, by apostles or possibly appointed by elders (1 Timothy 4:14) to take care of ministering in physical things, especially charity for needy, although they too could have spiritual gifts; note Stephen and Philip (Acts 6:1-6; 1 Timothy 3:8-13).

It is noteworthy that both Chafer (1948) and the *New Scofield Bible* warn that the examples of the New Testament are not to be used to form a rigid, new, "Leviticus-like" rule for organizing a local church (for example, the disciples of Troas met every first day to break bread and thus this should be law for us). There seem to be other churches that met and did not always break bread. Though today we must follow specific teachings on offices and procedures, when specifics are not given we must then move as God, in grace, leads us.

Some can have an office and also be gifted, such as a deacon who is an evangelist or a teacher.

Forms of government are three:

1. Episcopalian—bishop or church leader who has power, by virtue of his office, to direct local church.

2. Representative—represents authority of duly appointed representatives of local church, such as the presbytery of Presbyterian churches.

3. Congregational—final authority is local congregation.

In early church, all three of these forms were evident in various places and times. Early church recognized apostles. Representative government was in Jerusalem in Acts 15. As churches matured, it seemed that authority passed to local churches such as Antioch, etc. (Revelation 2, 3).

Ordinances

There are two clearly defined ordinances set out for the church to observe: baptism and the Lord's Supper. The Roman Catholic church adds a number of ordinances and calls them *sacraments*, thus implying that merit or righteousness is attained through practice of these rituals. Some Protestant churches add the practice of footwashing (John 13) as an ordinance. We see no Scriptural injunction to make footwashing into an ordinance, whereas it is obvious that baptism and the Lord's Supper are to be practiced by the local church.

Baptism (Believer's Baptism)

The word *baptism*, taken from the Greek, means "to dip," "immerse," or "submerge." There are a number of Scriptural baptisms, under the categories of (1) real or actual baptisms and (2) ritual baptisms. *Ritual baptism* is to be done because the recipient wishes to testify that he or she believes a certain spiritual truth; however, the recipient does not gain any supernatural benefit by being baptized.

- Actual baptisms:
  - Baptism of the Holy Spirit (Acts 1:5; Romans 6:3, 4; 1 Corinthians 12:13; Galatians 3:26-28; Ephesians 4:5; Colossians 2:12). This was introduced into the church age at Pentecost and happens instantaneously to the believer at salvation, when the Christian is literally placed into (baptized) Christ.
  - Baptism of the cross (Matthew 20:22; Luke 12:50), when Christ literally became sin for us.
  - Baptism of Moses (when Moses lived and identified with Israel).

◦ Ritual baptisms:
- ◦ Baptism of John (Matthew 3:1-11; John 1:25-33). Candidate signified belief that Israel had sinned and recognized need for salvation for Israel only through coming of Messiah.
- ◦ Baptism of Jesus (Matthew 3:13-17). None others like it; a singular event as example to believers.
- ◦ Christian or believer's baptism (Acts 2:41, 9:18, 10:47, 48). Candidate is a believer testifying by baptism as to his or her previous act of faith of accepting Christ as Savior. It in no way imputes righteousness or is a part of salvation.

The symbolism of Christian baptism is fourfold:

1. Death and resurrection of Christ (Colossians 3:12; Romans 6:3, 4). References are to real Spirit baptism, but still teach typology of Christian baptism.

2. Believer's identification with Christ (1 Corinthians 12:13).

3. Believer's deliverance from power of sin—newness of life (Romans 6:4).

4. Picture of union of all believers in Christ (1 Corinthians 12:13).

Christians are to be baptized for at least two reasons:

1. To be obedient (Matthew 28:9).

2. As testimony to others of our faith in Christ.

The mode of baptism is by immersion because:

◦ Of the primary meaning of word *baptizo*.

◦ Christ, our example, was immersed.

◦ Of testimony of early church and writings, in which baptism was done by immersion.

◦ Of symbolism (images of death, burial, and resurrection strengthened by immersion).

Those who advocate the affusionist mode (baptism by sprinkling or pouring) feel symbolism is of Holy Spirit coming upon candidate; therefore, that mode makes sense. We feel that it is error to use this mode, but it does not seem major unless babies are baptized or the baptizers imply that the ritual brings salvation (baptismal regeneration).

Lord's Supper (2 Corinthians 11:23-28)

The Lord's Supper was originated by Christ at Passover and commanded by God to be carried on thereafter (Matthew 26:27).

Believers only should participate. Some think that only baptized believers should participate, because baptism is a symbol of commencing the new life and the Lord's Supper is a symbol of the sustaining power of that new life. A person is baptized once (as he is saved once) but takes part in the Lord's Supper often (1 John 1:9); picture of cleansing often and enjoying fellowship with Christ as a result.

How long and how often to be partaken of? "Till He comes"; "As oft as ye do it" (1 Corinthians 11:26)—no set rule, though some say at every meeting.

Why? A time of purifying in life of believer; "examine yourself" (1 Corinthians 11), although confession of believer's sin is not to be done exclusively at that time. Every participant should participate as one who is regarding not iniquity and is in fellowship with the Lord—or else judgments of 1 Corinthians 11:28-32 take place.

Three interpretations of Lord's Supper:

1. Transubstantiation (Roman Catholic)—bread and wine become actual body and blood of Christ at time of priest's consecration of elements. We reject this view because it would mean that Christ is being crucified afresh, dying again—anti-Scriptural.

2. Consubstantiation (Lutherans and Church of England)—while bread and wine remain such in actuality, the body and blood are present in a spiritual sense and present only at moment they are partaken of; after being taken, they cease to be body and blood.

3. Symbolism—bread and wine are only symbols of Christ's body ("This do in remembrance of Me").

Discipline

The church is under grace rather than law; nevertheless, in the church age there is a problem of carnality in the believer and believers living out of fellowship in the flesh. Therefore, we find the Lord has laid down steps for keeping the church clean and her testimony strong before the world (Titus 2:14). The steps of church discipline are:

- ஃ Judgment of self (1 Corinthians 11:31; 1 John 1:9). When the believer, through the Spirit and the Word, knows he has sinned and is out of fellowship with the Lord, he is to restore fellowship by confessing that sin.

- ஃ Judgment by the church. If the sinning brother will not judge himself, then he must be judged by the local church (1 Corinthians 5:11, 12; Galatians 6:1), in a process whereby the erring brother is encouraged to deal with his sin. This introduces the principles of Matthew 18: 15-17. Also, the purpose is to get an erring brother back into a working relationship to the church and in fellowship with the Lord.

- ஃ Judgment by God. God's judgment comes in time. If the fallen brother does not judge himself, nor respond to the discipline of the church, or if the church does not discipline him, then God will judge or chastise that individual in time as well as after death (Hebrews 12:5-13; 1 Corinthians 11:32).

Reward of the Local Church

There are numerous judgments in Scripture. Some are for believers, others for Israel, gentile nations, Satan, and the lost peoples of earth. The believer is never to be condemned for sin, as that judgment was taken by Christ on the cross when He was judged, and paid, for our sins. Since Christ has already paid for our sins, we'll never have to face judgment for sin (John 3:18, 5:24, 6:37; Romans 5:1, 8:1; 1 Corinthians 11:32). In his standing the Christian is righteous; however, he must account for his daily walk and service before the Lord, and that account is before the judgment seat of Christ (Romans 14:10; 2 Corinthians 5:10; Ephesians 6:8).

There are three major figures in Scripture to denote the nature of the believer's rewards at the judgment seat:

1. Figure of stewardship (Romans 14:10-12). This judgment refers to the value or quality of life; in this passage the Christian is looked upon as a steward or trustee.

2. Figure of a building built upon the foundation of Christ (1 Corinthians 3:9-15). Each believer is building, for himself, upon Christ, the foundation provided by grace. This is not character building as described in fruits of Spirit (Galatians 5:23, 24), but rather refers to service or works that shall be tested by God's judgment fire. Every lasting work (that done under leadership of Spirit) is purified and saved; every work done in flesh (for fleshly reasons when out of fellowship) is burned up and lost for eternity.

3. Figure of race and winning prize (1 Corinthians 9:16-27). Refers to quality of Christian life and service. Paul talks of his own faithfulness in works (18–23) and says that the Christian should exert all his strength that he may obtain his full reward. Half-hearted effort brings less reward; no effort eventually results in a casting away (or disapproval) or loss of ministry. This passage talks of a temperate life under control and presented to God (Romans 12:1, 2).

Rewards are referred to as crowns or prizes that represent five distinct forms of service and suffering. The Christian is warned lest he lose his reward (Colossians 2:18; 2 John 8; Revelation 3:11). The crowns are:

1. Incorruptible crown—for those who honor precepts of Bible (1 Corinthians 9:25).

2. Crown of rejoicing—for soul winners and those involved in missionary effort (1 Thessalonians 2:19).

3. Crown of life—for faithful endurance under severe trials (James 1:12).

4. Crown of righteousness—for those who kept faith and love His appearing (2 Timothy 4:8).

5. Crown of glory—for each Christian who has fed his flock and been an example thereto (1 Peter 5:1-4, 6).

All may be lost by failure to hold fast in this life (Revelation 3:11).

The crowns will be cast at Jesus' feet (Revelation 4:10), which of course shows that we will be close to Him in eternity. The probability is that the reward for faithful service will be a privileged place of service in heaven (Revelation 22:3). This will be the ultimate joy and intimacy beyond our comprehension. Probably those who do not work here will be placed in other service not so close to Christ. The principle of Matthew 25:14-30 (parable of talents) may apply here. "Faithfulness in our service here will result in privileges of service in eternity" (Chafer, vol. 4, 1948).

Angelology
Doctrine of Angels

❦

INTRODUCTION

The order of celestial beings called *angels* is mentioned in the Old Testament at least 108 times and in the New Testament 165 times. They are distinct from humanity and the Godhead, and are important enough to be mentioned often and have much information dispensed concerning them. In these references, we recognize that the Hebrew word *mal'ak* and the Greek word *angelos* both mean "messenger"; occasionally there are references to human messengers, but the ones we are interested in here refer to a special, created class of celestial beings that we will refer to as *angels*.

God created five divisions of finite beings:

1. Angels
2. Fallen angels
3. Gentiles
4. Jews
5. Christians (invisible church)

Consequently, if we are to be fairly well informed of Scriptural truths, we must take time to study all five of these groups. We have previously studied three (gentiles, Jews, and Christians); now we will study the first two.

Here is an outline of our angelology study:
    Reality of the existence of angels
        Creation and mode of existence
        Sphere or home of angels
    Description of angels
        Personality of angels
        Number of angels
        Power of angels
        Progress of angels
        Other characteristics of angels
        Classifications or delineation of angels
    Importance of elect angels to men
        Ministry of angels
        Spectators of humanity
    Satanology, demonology, and the invisible war
        Does Satan exist? Do demons exist? Why study Satan and
          demonism? The invisible war
        How did Satan come into existence?
        Pre-earth history
        History after appearance on earth
        Present-day activities of Satan
        Limitations of Satan
        Final disposition of Satan
        Conclusions regarding Satan

I. REALITY OF THE EXISTENCE OF ANGELS

Angels are living beings of high position and great consequence in the world. Some are good and some are bad, as we shall see. All were created by God and are involved in tremendous issues with Him. We have not been briefed on all of the past history or the plans of the future; complete disclosure has been withheld, but we know enough to see that angels are very important in God's plans. Some Scriptural verses that refer to angels are Matthew 25:41; Psalms 104:4, 34:7, 8:4, 5; Malachi 3:1; plus others.

Creation and Mode of Existence

> Colossians 1:16, 17 implies that all angels were created simultaneously; creation of angels was completed at that time and none will be added later on; each was a direct creation of God.

> They are eternal (will never cease to exist) and do not marry (Matthew 22:28-30), therefore do not have families or reproduce. They are totally responsible to their Creator as it says in Colossians 1:16, 17: "by Christ and for Christ."

> They will not and cannot die (1 Corinthians 15:25, 26). They exist with embodiment but not as mortal humans or animals; rather, as a localized, determinate spiritual form with personality (intelligence) and a ministry (1 Corinthians 15:39, 40), celestial (heavenly) and/or terrestrial (earthly). To human beings, their appearance varies, so they look like men on occasion (Hebrews 13:2) and glorious on other occasions (Matthew 28:2-4). They exist in a spiritual body (Luke 24:37-39: "hath not flesh and bones as ye see me have"), and are able to pass from one locality to another with incredible speed (Daniel 9:21), but are corporeal (pertaining to matter/body) (John 20:12; Genesis 18:1-8, 19:1-3).

Sphere or Home of Angels

Mark 13:32 asserts that angels inhabit heavenly spheres (also Galatians 1:8: "though an angel from heaven"; Ephesians 3:15; Matthew 6:10). Hebrew word for *heaven* is plural, indicating three heavens, as Moses made tabernacle with three parts (Hebrews 8:5). Other references: Matthew 18:10; Luke 2:13-15; John 1:15; Revelation 5:11, 7:11.

II. DESCRIPTION OF ANGELS

Personality of Angels

Angels are not impersonal influences, such as thoughts or ideas emanating from God, nor their appearance just visions in someone's mind. Rather, they are personal beings. Satan (a fallen angel) is described in 2 Timothy 2:25, 26 as one who has a will. See 2 Samuel 14:20; Revelation 12:9, 12, 22:8, 9.

Number of Angels

The number of angels is innumerable; we know only that it is a vast amount, but a set number, as they do not reproduce or die (Hebrews 12:22; Matthew 26:53; Daniel 7:10; Psalms 118:17; 2 Kings 6:17; Revelation 5:12).

Power of Angels

The power of angels, derived from God, is great even though restricted. They are not omnipotent. They are stronger than human beings. For example, man can thwart the influence of evil spirits only by divine enablement (Ephesians 6:10-12; 1 John 4:4), but even angels call for assistance when in battle with another angel (Jude 1:9). Adjectives such as "mighty," "strong," and "powerful" abound in Scriptural descriptions of angels. Mighty deeds are done, such as the death of all the firstborn in Egypt by one death angel.

Progress of Angels

Progress simply means that angels do learn or develop, for Scripture describes them in many places as learning while observing humans, especially the outworking of redemption. They are not omniscient (1 Peter 1:12; Ephesians 3:10), but learn the manifold wisdom of God.

Other Characteristics of Angels

They are masculine; always described in masculine gender (Mark 16:5, 6; Matthew 28:2-4; Luke 1:26); celibate (Matthew 22:30); subordinate and subject to God. Also immutable (unchanging) and *illoco* (able to move about).

Classifications of Angels

The Bible, which doesn't indulge in tautology or useless information, refers to five groups of angels: (1) thrones—those who sit in ruling capacity; (2) dominions—those who rule specific areas; (3) principalities—those who govern; (4) powers—those who exercise power; and (5) authorities—those given special responsibility (Daniel 9:21, 22). There are also two special categories:

1. Elect, holy, for good angels (1 Timothy 5:21; Hebrews 1:6; Isaiah 6:3; John 12:41; Revelation 5:11, 12). These are further divided into:

   ❧ Cherubim, who appear to be involved with God's holiness in opposition to sin (Genesis 3:22-24; Exodus 26:1; Ezekiel).

   ❧ Seraphim—only Isaiah 6:2-7 deals with uncleanness in God's people and preparing them for God. Both express respect to divine holiness. These angels are living creatures—vivid, full, unceasingly active in worshipping God (Revelation 4:6-9).

   Some individual archangels are named: Lucifer the fallen one; Michael—seemingly in charge of Jews (Daniel 12:1; Jude 1:9); and Gabriel—the "mighty one" who carried out God's special assignments (Daniel 9:21).

2. Fallen angels—angels that fell when some sided with Satan and battled God's host. They were created with free will and chose to follow the greatest angel, Lucifer, instead of God (Revelation 21:7-9; 2 Peter 2:4-6; Jude 6, 7; 1 Peter 3:19; Matthew 18:10, 13:9; 1 John 5:18).

   ❧ Free to follow Satan and harass God's creation temporarily.
      ↝ They obtain men's bodies (Luke 8:26-36).
      ↝ They vacate men's bodies (Matthew 12:43).
      ↝ They hurt men (Luke 4:35, 8:29, 9:42).

   ❧ Characteristics: some are deaf (Mark 9:14-29); dumb (Mark 9:17); lying (1 Kings 22:22); foul (Mark 9:25a);

seducing (1 Timothy 4:1); powerful (Mark 5:8-13; Luke 13:16).

- Speak through men's mouths and recognize Jesus.

- Evidence of their existence:
  - Four gospels refer to demonism as something well known; people showed no surprise at demonic possession.
  - Jews claimed to have cast out demons (Matthew 12:27).
  - Christ cast out demons and apostles came in contact with same (Matthew 10:1; Mark 16:17; Acts 8:7).
  - Demonism seen by missionaries today.

- Bound angels in Tartarus (2 Peter 2:4; Jude 6; Ephesians 6:12). Left first estate and became men who married on earth—no marriage in heaven, but earth not mentioned (Genesis 6); sons of God (Job 1, 2). *Note:* Demonic possession prolific before Flood; so shall it be at coming of Son of Man (Matthew 24:37). Tribulation will be demonic possession and intermarriage of demons and humans as Satan endeavors to control earth.

III. IMPORTANCE OF ELECT ANGELS TO MEN

Ministry of Angels

- They are faithful to serve mankind, not on basis of their love for humanity but in obedience to God.

- They reveal God's will to men (Hebrews 2:2; Daniel 8:16, 17; Luke 1:11-13; Acts 1:9-11).

- They help saints (Daniel 3:5; 2 Kings 6:15-18; Hebrews 1:14).

- They encourage saints (Acts 27:23-25).

- They free imprisoned saints (Acts 5:19, 20, 12:7-10).

- They sustain saints (Matthew 4:11).

- They conduct saints (Acts 8:26; Genesis 24:7; Exodus 23:20-23).

✦ They guard saints (Daniel 12:1; Hebrews 1:14).

✦ They are involved in welcoming believers to heaven (Luke 16:22).

✦ They brought law and assist God in communicating (Galatians 3:19; Hebrews 2:2).

✦ They accompany court (2 Thessalonians 1:7).

✦ They harvest at end of age (Matthew 13:30).

Spectators of Humanity

✦ Angels see and sometimes oversee human beings (Luke 15:10; Jude 1:24; Luke 12:8, 9; 1 Timothy 3:16; Revelation 14:10, 11).

✦ They saw creation also (Job 38:7); giving of law (Galatians 3:19); birth of Christ (Luke 2:13) and His temptation, resurrection, and ascension; will see His Second Coming.

IV. SATANOLOGY, DEMONOLOGY, AND THE INVISIBLE WAR

Does Satan Exist? Do Demons Exist? Why Study Satan and Demonism? The Invisible War

Scripture is clear (Ezekiel 28:11-27; Isaiah 14:12-17) that Satan does exist as a definite person; he is not merely a symbol of evil or a figure of speech. He is an angelic being of wide and powerful influence, created by God. Satan, because of pride, became the author of sin, a rebel against God, and enemy of humanity and God. He exists as the head of an empire antagonistic to God and His people, and becomes increasingly violent and desperate as his time and influence on earth draw to a close. We study him, his followers, his goals, and his eternal destiny so that we can know his goals, methods, and character and recognize his influence. By understanding our adversary, we become victorious through Christ.

The Bible teaches that two real, spiritual worlds exist, one good and the other evil. These two worlds are in direct conflict, each to the other, battling especially over humankind. The raging battle is an outright war in the spiritual realm: though invisible to the eyes of humanity, this war affects believers and the world.

How Did Satan Come into Existence?

Ezekiel 28:11-27 and Colossians 1:16 clearly teach that God created Lucifer in perfection.

Pre-earth History

All angels have functions (Ephesians 1:21); each has responsibilities and ministries, as described previously. Satan was created as the wisest and most beautiful angel, to minister directly in God's presence. Satan overlooked God, His throne, and all activity; he was doxology and was created to supervise all God's angelic creation. He evidently had great influence over angels (Ezekiel 28:11-27) "that covereth" (28:14) and hovered over God as cherubs in Holy of Holies.

Did an omnipotent, omniscient God know that Lucifer would fall? Of course. Why, then, did He create him? We don't know; we just accept.

Lucifer's pre-earth activities or assignments included:

- Covering God, ceaselessly giving praise, reflecting the glory of God, and administering God's wishes.

- Directing the other angels.

According to Isaiah 14:12-17, Lucifer decided to rebel against God as described in the five "I will's" of that passage. Note the description of his desires:

1. "I will ascend into heaven." There are three heavens; Lucifer wanted to ascend from the second heaven, his abode, and live in the third heaven where he served. His desire was to sit on the throne of God.

2. "I will exalt my throne above stars of God." Job 38:7 describes stars as angels, so Lucifer desired to usurp God's

authority over the entire angelic creation without submitting himself to the authority of the Creator.

3. "I will sit also upon mount"—wanted to control universe. Isaiah 2:2 shows that "mountain" is the right to rule.

4. "I will ascend above" (Exodus 16:10, 40:33; 1 Kings 8:10). Cloud was glory of God; Lucifer wanted greater glory than God.

5. "I will be like the Most High"—desired to be independent of God and possess God's authority and glory. Pride is same one every unsaved man seeks: "to be his own God"; yet both are totally unqualified for such a position.

Pre-earth Hierarchy (Ephesians 6:10-17)

ֿ◦ God began His work of creation in the angelic realm (Colossians 1:16).

ֿ◦ God created angels with personality and volition (Psalms 148:2); Scripture tells of those who chose to worship and have knowledge (Matthew 24:36) and will. Hebrews 1:14 says they were created to minister and have celestial bodies and were included in God's system of governing the universe (Daniel 12:1, 10:13).

ֿ◦ Revelation 12:4 gives us a clue of the extent of Satan's original rebellion against God. He was able, evidently, to persuade one-third of the angels that he could elevate himself and those who followed him. He organized a "God-like" system of hierarchy, ranks, etc., for Satan was never an originator but always an imitator.

ֿ◦ He planned a kingdom (Ephesians 6:12) with four ranks that correspond to those in Colossians 1:16. Followers of Satan we call demons. The demons are innumerable.

ֿ◦ The child of God is surrounded by fallen angels and guardian angels. The demons are assigned to frustrate the will of God for us as God's children and are faithful ministers of Satan, for they were made to serve. Demons arrange things and circumstances to make us fall; the guardian angels watch over our physical bodies (Hebrews 1:14), and God gives us weapons to defeat Satan's demonic plans (Ephesians 6:10-20).

Matthew 17:14-21 describes some of the satanic activity that we will introduce in the next section.

History After Appearance on Earth

Appearance on Earth (Genesis 3:1-7)

- ✎ God created man in His own image as God's administrator over the earth (Genesis 1:26). According to Revelation 12:4, Satan decided to make earth his kingdom, and to establish his realm independent of God; thus, he had to depose and destroy man, who was in God's image.

- ✎ Satan cannot materialize his body, which was suited for heavenly existence, and so must appropriate a physical body through which to work—thus, the serpent became his embodiment. Naïve Eve was probably surprised to encounter a talking animal, but just accepted it as another of the great creations and revelations that she enjoyed every day in Eden. God is so original that we'll be enjoying His surprises throughout eternity. Later, in Genesis 6, Satan appropriated many human bodies and infiltrated the human race as men gave their bodies over to him. It seems that each demon who goes so far as to inhabit a human body, upon release from that body, is chained immediately in lower hell (Tartarus) (Jude 6-8).

- ✎ Purpose is to destroy God's creation by destroying God's Holy Name and promises. This is obvious by:
  - ↬ His appearance in the Garden.
  - ↬ His infiltration of the human race before the time of Noah.
  - ↬ Babel, Cain, and attacks on Job, David, Christ, Peter, etc.

Description of Satan

- Called Lucifer, Son of the Morning, created in perfect beauty (Ezekiel 28:12, 17) and great brilliance. Some say he was the choir leader in heaven, as tabrets and pipes were prepared in him the day he was created (Ezekiel 28:13). Described as an "angel of light" (2 Corinthians 11:14); he is a person even as Christ is a person. He is very attractive to human beings.

- His fall came because of pride (Isaiah 14:14); choosing his own will over God's.

- Many names attributed to him in Bible:
  - Angel of light (2 Corinthians 11:14).
  - Rebel (Job 1:13-22).
  - Satan—adversary, hater, and accuser (1 Chronicles 21:1).
  - Devil—slanderer, accuser, deceiver (Revelation 20:2).
  - Beelzebub—prince of demons (Mark 3:22).
  - Belial—"good for nothing" (Deuteronomy 13:13).
  - The Wicked One (1 John 2:14).
  - The evil one (1 John 5:18).
  - Old serpent (Revelation 12:3, 9, 20:2).
  - Dragon (Revelation 20:2).
  - Prince of this world—politics, business, and society are under him (Matthew 4; Luke 4).
  - Ruler of darkness (Ephesians 6:12).
  - God of this age (2 Corinthians 4:4).
  - Prince of power of air (Ephesians 2:2).
  - Father of lies (John 8:44).
  - Murderer (John 8:44; 1 John 3:12-15).
  - Roaring lion (1 Peter 5:8).
  - Adversary (1 Peter 5:8).
  - Lawless one (2 Thessalonians 2:1-12).

With such an abundance of references and descriptions given over to Satan, let's not say that he is unimportant, incidental, or that we have not been instructed concerning him. We must take him seriously.

Activities and Strategies of Satan's Warfare against God

- Doubt and denial of God's Word (Genesis 3:1-5; John 8:44).
- Threefold temptation (Matthew 4:1-11):
  - Endeavoring to induce Christ to act independent of Father or to depart from will of God. Hunger in this case was God's will for Christ. Satan said since you are Son, cannot you do what you want?
  - Endeavoring to challenge Christ to doubt work of God— test His promises to see if God really means what He says, as was done to Eve in Garden (Matthew 4:5, 6).
  - Offering power on earth now through wrong channels— thus recognizing power of Satan and diverting worship of God to himself; this is the ultimate temptation (Matthew 4:8).
- Invitation to sin (1 John 2:7-17). It is a comfort to know that Satan cannot attack through a multitude of channels, but rather only three channels as described in this passage—all sins fall into one of these three classifications:
  - Gate One—"Lust of the flesh." This sin recognizes that man, in Adam, is possessed by a nature that is fleshly. Its appetites, cravings, desires, and passions are natural to a man living in his natural state or in carnality. Three other terms used to describe these areas are "world, flesh, and devil." This is sin of flesh; to defeat this sin, RUN! FLEE! (2 Timothy 2:19-22).
  - Gate Two—"Lust of the eye." This sin recognizes that man is not only carnal (Gate One) but is also basically selfish— that what he sees he covets and seeks to attain for himself. This is also called "sin of world." To defeat this sin we must focus on Christ, not the world. Instructions are found in Philippians 1:21, 2:3, 4, 3:20, 4:4-7.
  - Gate Three—"Pride of life." Sins that appeal to pride; loves and strives for that which elevates and promotes self and gives a sense of independence to the individual. This is also called "sin of the devil," who is originator of pride. The Scriptural attack on this sin is found in James 4:7, 8,

where it tells us to "submit to God and resist the devil." Note a different response through the Word to each attack of Satan to render us ineffective for God.

- Satan tries to reach an individual through one or more of the three gates, knowing that as the individual succumbs he will become disobedient to God and love the sin; what a man loves he will obey and follow—namely, Satan. His process is slow, planting the seed and then nurturing it through life; only God's Word through the Spirit is able to root out these weeds.

- An individual facing temptation can analyze it to see which category the sin falls into and then use Word of God, energized by Spirit, to meet the attack. During Christ's temptation in area of flesh, He answered, "man shall not live by bread alone but by the Word of God." In area of "eyes," He said, "worship the Lord thy God and Him only shalt thou see"—focus on the Lord only. In area of selfishness, He said, "I am willing to wait God's time." Answer is to know that God gives answer to every specific sin in His Word. Find it and apply it.

Remember steps to downfall as illustrated by David in 2 Samuel 11. He saw, he desired, and then he took. Mind saw, heart lusted, and will disobeyed Word of God. Cut it off before it reaches fruition by staying faithful to Word and obeying. How? Apply Philippians 4:8.

- Opposition to preaching (Matthew 13:1-11).

- Deception (1 Timothy 4:1-8).

- Perversion (1 Timothy 4:3, 4)—distorter of wine, food, etc.

- Imitation or beguiling (2 Corinthians 11:1-15).

- Lawlessness (2 Thessalonians 2:1-12: "the lawless one"); rebellion (Job 1:13-22).

- Adversary (1 Peter 5:8).

- Further strategies against God and the believer, as described in Scripture as the work of Satan.

- He produces sickness and has power of death (Hebrews 2:14; Luke 13:16; Acts 10:38).
- He lays snares for men (2 Timothy 2:26).
- He takes Word out of hearts (Matthew 13–19).
- He puts wicked purposes into hearts (Ephesians 4:27).
- He blinds minds (2 Corinthians 4:4).
- He harasses men (2 Corinthians 12:7).
- He accuses men before God (Revelation 12:10).
- He enters into men (John 13:2).
- He sows tares among God's people (Matthew 13:38, 39).
- He gives power to lawless ones (2 Corinthians 2:10, 11).
- He resists God's servants (Zechariah 3:1; Daniel 10:13).
- He hinders God's servants (1 Thessalonians 2:18).
- He sifts God's servants (Luke 22:31).
- He holds the world (1 John 5:19).

Present-Day Activities of Satan

- Control of the world system. As prince of the earth, we must recognize that Satan will utilize every facet of the world to attack the Lord and His people, especially in the following areas (list not exhaustive):
  - Family.
  - Marriage.
  - Governments—nations—influence over world events (Daniel 10).
  - Teaching, education, philosophy, through teachers, philosophers, educators.
  - Science.
  - Industry—inventions and implements of evil manufacturers as well as multitudes of sophisticated toys and distractions.
  - Pleasures—materials for soft and lengthy life without God.
  - Media.
- Spiritism (Deuteronomy 18:9-11; Leviticus 20:27; 1 Samuel 28:7-25).
  - Bible never indicates possibility of receiving messages from dead through mediums and Old Testament

condemns efforts to do so. Bishop Pike was deceived by mediums who were tools of great deceiver. Spiritism or mediums described as necromancers (receiving messages from dead) who write automatically, produce music on invisible instruments, or produce voices of dead are imposters using mechanical means; others seem to have satanic power (Koch, 1962); Christians are to avoid such.

- Fortune telling (tea leaves, palms, crystal balls, cards, astrology, or whatever) attempts to discern the future outside of God's Word. Description in 2 Corinthians 11:13-15 and Deuteronomy 18:10-12 of people who have special power from God to foretell future with a gift of prophecy, but difficult to distinguish divine rather than demonic influence. *Answer:* Deuteronomy 18:21, 22; believers should avoid them (Isaiah 47:11-15; 1 Corinthians 14:37; Revelation 22:18, 19).

- Witchcraft and Satanism—groups of Satan worshippers can be found worldwide. Old Testament word for witchcraft is *Kashaph*, which means sorcerer or one who uses magical formulas, incantations, mutterings to exercise control over unseen world. Not all magic is illusion or sleight-of-hand hocus-pocus, according to Bible; read of Pharaoh's diviners in Exodus 7, 8. Be careful!

- Demonic possession—for details, read a book such as Merrill Unger's *Demons in the World Today* (1972).
  - Demonic possession is a condition in which one or more evil spirits inhabit the body of a human being and take complete control of the victim at will. Possessed persons' symptoms vary: some are depressive and melancholy; others are ferocious or ecstatic during attacks. They appear healthy and normal in between attacks.
  - Distinguishing marks of demonic possession are automatic projection of a new personality in victim; a different voice, language and dialect, and pronouns indicate new personality. Read examples in Unger's book (1972).
  - Demonic possession is not uncommon in undeveloped, unenlightened countries. Missionaries often have contact

with such people. There have been reported instances in America today as well, as documented in Unger's book.

- I believe that a believer can never become demon-possessed, because indwelling Spirit will never be removed from believer. However, Unger (1972, p. 116) claims that missionaries in dark countries have seen new believer delivered from demonic possession become repossessed and return to idolatry. This is experiential evidence; I would disagree that it is possible because of our salvation, which includes new creation and indwelling Spirit, and feel the Lord would take a believer home first (1 John 5: sin unto death). Satan cannot touch our salvation or God's love for us (Romans 8:38, 39).

- Exorcism (cleansing of demons) and deliverance from the slavery of the occult is certainly Biblical. Christ cleansed men from demonic possession, as did His disciples, though they also failed. It can be accomplished by the power and command of Christ coming through a Spirit-filled believer who is led to deliver such a person. In fact, if the church does not do this, who is going to deliver the world from the power of Satan? We must provide the spiritual leadership and faith to deliver the world from the power of sin and give the message of salvation. We are not to be fearful, but serve in the power of the Lord. Only as we are knowledgeable of Scripture, obedient to the Word, and hospitable to the indwelling Spirit can this be accomplished—but we do have the power, through Christ, to exorcise and deliver people from the power of sin (Matthew 10:1; Mark 16:17; Luke 19:1; Acts16:18; 19:12).

Unger describes prayer battles of great length and intensity, sometimes going on for days or weeks and often recruiting other believers, but today God can cleanse through believers. The cleansing comes when "confesses Christ as Saviour ... and confesses sins of occult involvement." Liberation then comes through greatness of God's power.

- Healing and false religions may be Satan's delusions (Mark 13:22; 2 Thessalonians 2:7; 1 Timothy 4:1).

Limitations of Satan

- He is not omnipresent (Luke 10:18). He moves rapidly to help agents, but is not everywhere.

- He is not omniscient—angels still learn, and he is an angel.

- He is not omnipotent—He is subject to Word of God (Job 1, 2).

- Believers have authority over Satan (Ephesians 2:1-10, 1:20-22).

- Believers can put Satan to flight (James 4:1-10).

Warnings to Believers

- Do not traffic with demons (Deuteronomy 18:9-11).

- Areas to watch—occult, spiritism, and all ramifications of Satan's modern and ancient techniques of attack upon the Lord's people.

Defense of Believers against Satan and Demons

- Recall:
  - Power of Satan. Don't regard him lightly, though he is sovereignly restricted—he can do only what God permits as God carries him down to defeat (Job 1:12, 2:6; 1 John 4:4). He cannot touch our salvation or separate us from the love of God (Romans 8:38, 39).
  - That Satan's devices and schemes are taught in Scripture; become aware of them (2 Corinthians 2:11; Ephesians 6:11).
  - That Christians are victorious in Christ, which means Satan is defeated—positional truth (Romans 8:1; Ephesians 1:6; Hebrews 2:14, 15).
  - That God uses Satan (2 Corinthians 12:7-10; Job) and keeps saints (2 Thessalonians 3:3; Romans 8:28-30, 38, 39).
- Resist—an attitude of our life (Ephesians 4:27):
  - By donning armor provided by God (Ephesians 6:10-18).
  - In submission to God (James 4:4-10).

- Positive Godly action—pray for deliverance (Matthew 6:13, 26:41); protection (2 Thessalonians 3:1, 2, etc.).

- Rely on power, providence, and promises of God. We are victors in Him (Ephesians 1:20-23; Philippians 2:9, 10).

- Vigilance to be exercised by believer (1 Peter 5:8; 2 Corinthians 2:11).

Final Disposition of Satan

CHRIST WILL CONQUER SATAN (COLOSSIANS 2:9-17):

- In temptation time (Matthew 4:1-11).

- By casting out demons (Matthew 4:24, 8:31; Mark 1:23, 5:2; Luke 9:42, 11:20, 13:32).

- In end time of judgment (Jude 6; Revelation 20:10; Matthew 25:41).

SATAN'S FINAL DESTINY (REVELATION 20:1-10):

- Satan has already fallen morally and is separated from God (Ezekiel 28:15; 1 Timothy 3:6).

- God's perfect judgment has been secured at the cross (John 12:31, 16:11; Colossians 2:14, 15). The sentence on Satan will be completed in future.

- Satan will be cast out of heaven in midst of tribulation and as a result of war in heaven. He will then be limited to earth (Revelation 12:7-12; Isaiah 14:12; Luke 10:18).

- Satan will be confined to bottomless pit for 1,000 years (Revelation 20:1-3, 7) to stop him from deceiving the nations.

- Then to final destination, the lake of fire at end of millennium, after short season of rebellion, to prove his real "mettle" (Revelation 20:10).

Conclusions Regarding Satan

- Satan and his evil spirits will use every device possible, as described in Scripture, to hurt God's children, embarrass God, and delay Satan's inevitable detention in the lake of fire.

- Satan is unable to harm the believer, if that person accepts the instruction of the Bible, maintains a life of prayer, submits himself to God, and resists the Devil.

Eschatology
Doctrine of Last Times or Things to Come

INTRODUCTION

The early church obviously was very interested in the doctrine of the return of Christ. In fact, 1 and 2 Thessalonians place great emphasis on the theme of the return of Christ, which is referred to as the "Blessed Hope" in 1 John. The early generations kept this truth alive, but it seems that from Constantine's time (AD 300) on, until the late twentieth century, this doctrine was neglected and rejected.

In the past hundred years or so, this doctrine has been restored to many, although there is still much opposition in many circles to the doctrine of Christ's return. According to 2 Peter 3:4, even this indifference is Scriptural. There are four reasons for opposition:

1. Date setters have brought great disrepute to this precious doctrine.

2. Unscriptural doctrines taught by many advocates of this doctrine—annihilation, probationism, etc.

3. Preconceived notions and prejudices; some Scripture has been interpreted wrongly for so many years that erroneous teachings mask the truth.

4. Unregenerated hearts make fun of this doctrine (2 Peter 3:4).

Yet this doctrine is not only alive but important, because:

- ✤ Its prominence in Scripture (more than 300 references in New Testament and countless times in Old Testament).

- ✤ It is a key to Scripture—many passages can never be understood if not interpreted in light of this doctrine (Exodus, Enoch, Noah's day, Isaac and Rebekah, Psalms, Old Testament, New Testament, and covenants and promises).

- ✤ It is the hope of our church and age.

- ✤ It is the incentive for Biblical Christianity.

- ✤ It has marked effect on our service.

The outline of our study is as follows:
Physical death
Bodily resurrection and other resurrections
Intermediate state of the believer
Rapture
Tribulation
Specifics on the beast
Specifics on the false prophet
Armageddon
Second Coming of Christ
The Resurrections
Judgments of the End Time
The glorious age of the Millennium
The last state of the wicked
After the Millennium
Eternal final state of the believers

I. PHYSICAL DEATH

- ✤ Introduced in story of creation.

- ✤ Romans 5:12 tells us that death has passed upon all men. This refers to physical death. All men die physically unless the Lord returns to intervene in their lives. But humans are extremely uncomfortable in the presence of death and fear it for a number of reasons, one of which is that God never created man to die—consequently, it is contrary to divine plan. Sin brought death and the grave and removed humanity from the fulfillment of God's plan for humankind.

- Scripture teaches that physical death is not the cessation of being, but merely the transfer of the soul to an eternal abiding place.
  - The Christian has a reservation in the presence of the Lord (1 Peter 1:4; Philippians 1:23; 2 Corinthians 5:8). Word *present* means "to be at home with." The Christian goes home.
  - The ungodly are set aside for judgment (2 Peter 2:9) and will eventually reside in the lake of fire (Revelation 20:15).
- Death is not soul sleep—in Scripture, *sleep* when referring to death refers to the believer in rest; the believer is not in an unconscious state, but awake and waiting for the consummation of God's plan; transfiguration (Revelation 6:9, 10; Luke 16; Philippians 1:21).
- Death means separation, life means union (Romans 8:35-39; Philippians 1:21).
- The six deaths of Scripture are:
  - Physical—Separation of body from soul and spirit (Lazarus) (2 Corinthians 5:1-8).
  - Second death—Separation from God in eternity (Revelation 20:13; Hebrews 9:27).
  - Spiritual death—Separation from God in time—lostness (2 Corinthians 15:22; Romans 6:23).
  - Christian's personal death—identified with Christ is His death (Galatians 2:20; Romans 6:1-4).
  - Christian experiential death—loss of fellowship because of sin, carnality (Romans 8:6; Ephesians 5:14; 1 Timothy 5:6).
  - Sexual death—impotence (Abraham) (Romans 4:17, 19; Hebrews 11:12).

II. BODILY RESURRECTION AND OTHER RESURRECTIONS

Bodily Resurrection

The Christian's bodily resurrection is certain—"And we shall be changed" (1 Corinthians 15:52c). We shall have the same body with a great transformation as we see in the resurrected body of Christ, able to penetrate solids but with the print of the nails. A wheat germ produces wheat, a lily a lily, etc.

- 1 Corinthians 15:42-44 describes the resurrection of the just (God says nothing of the bodies of the lost in their state of eternal death).

- The believer's resurrected body will be like Christ's resurrected body (Philippians 3:20, 21; 1 John 3:1, 2).

The fact of resurrection is anticipated in the Old Testament, where we constantly hear such terms as "awake and live" (Isaiah 26:19; Job 19:26, 27; Psalms 16:9, 11; Daniel 6:73, 12:2) and see many types of that truth:

- Joseph in pit, counted dead but brought back alive to his father.

- Jonah in belly of fish for three days.

- Daniel came out alive from lion's den.

- Shadrach, Meshek, and Abednego.

This truth is also revealed in the New Testament (1 Corinthians 15:22; Acts 24:15; Matthew 22:30-32; Luke 14:13, 14; 1 Thessalonians 4:14-16; 2 Timothy 1:10).

Nature of Resurrection

Theories Proposed in Contrast to Scriptural Declaration (per Cambron)

- Germ theory—Jewish—in Talmud a little bone called *luz* which death can't destroy, out of which body is resurrected.

- Islamic "identity theory"—raised as buried. An infant will be an infant, a lunatic a lunatic, person with an arm missing will be raised with arm missing, etc. If true, we would not be like Jesus.

- Reincarnation theory—at death we go immediately into another body. If so, we would not be "at home" with the Lord.

- Intermediate body theory—new body immediately upon death. Based on 2 Corinthians 5:1-4, but this Scriptural passage refers only to believers alive at Rapture.

Resurrection According to Scripture

- Scripture says that we, at death, are transferred immediately into the presence of the Lord in an intermediate state (see next section) awaiting consummation of God's program, which includes the joining of our soul and spirit to the resurrected body.

- The time of the resurrection. The first resurrection includes Christ and all believers of all ages at different intervals. First Christ, then Church at Rapture before Tribulation, then the Old Testament and Tribulation saints after the Tribulation (1 Corinthians 15:20; Daniel 12:1, 2, 13).

Other Scriptural Resurrections

- Resurrection of Jesus Christ—First resurrection.
  - Prophesied in Old Testament (Psalms 16:9, 10).
  - Described historically in gospels and verified by appearances.
  - Theological implications dealt with in New Testament beginning in Acts and climaxed in 1 Corinthians 15.
- Resurrection of saints in Jerusalem (Matthew 27:52, 53). No explanation given. Appears that graves were opened at death of Christ but bodies not raised unto Christ when He, the first-fruit, was raised three days later. Some feel there were very few involved, others more. Some think that because

these saints were resurrected with Christ, they were caught up to heaven; others feel they were "resuscitated" like Lazarus and eventually died again. Scripture is not clear on this matter.

🙢 Resurrection of the church (Rapture)—see later section on the Rapture. The Rapture is the time at the end of the church age when Christ returns for His own; meets them, living and dead, in the air; and returns with both resurrected and transformed saints in their resurrected bodies (1 Thessalonians 4:13-18; 1 Corinthians 15:51-58; 1 John 3:2).

🙢 Resurrection of Old Testament saints—will be accomplished after the Tribulation at the time of Christ's return to earth to establish the Millennium. The group will include Old Testament and Tribulation saints (Daniel 12:1, 2; Isaiah 26:19-21).

🙢 Resurrection of Tribulation saints—as described above. Special mention of those who died as martyrs during Tribulation is found in Revelation 20:4, 5.

🙢 Resurrection of Millennial saints—Scripture is silent on this. We can only surmise from Isaiah 65:20 that there is aging and possible death during the Millennium. If so, they will be raised from the dead and taken with saints from earth while earth is being destroyed and rebuilt for eternity.

🙢 Resurrection of the wicked (Revelation 20:11-15)—the final resurrection before the creation of the new heavens and earth. Described in Daniel 12:2; Jude 23; Revelation 20:11-15.

III. Intermediate State of the Believer (State of Man Between Death and Resurrection)

Various words are used to describe the locale of the individual after death.

🙢 *Sheol* (Hebrew) and *Hades* (Greek)—place of departed souls and spirits. The mistranslation of these words in the King James Version has caused much trouble, as they were translated to mean "hell"—place of everlasting punishment—or "grave," "pit," and the like. Some have been led to believe that the grave is the only hell. According to Cambron (1947–1948), we must remember that:

~ These words are never found in plural form.

~ Sheol and Hades are never found on the face of the earth.

~ The Bible never speaks of an individual's Sheol.

~ Man never puts anyone in it, as in a grave.

~ Man never digs or makes a Sheol or Hades.

~ Bible never speaks of man touching Sheol.

~ Bible never speaks of a body going into Sheol except one time (Numbers 16:28-33), which proves the rule.

~ *Gehenna*—Greek word referring to fiery garbage pit outside walls of Jerusalem, but also refers to lake of fire (eternal abode of damned).

~ *Tartarus*—Greek word to describe lowest, vilest part of hell where certain rebellious demons are chained.

~ Hades/Sheol has two compartments, according to Luke 16:
~ Abraham's bosom—place of believing dead in Hades before Christ's death on cross.
~ Paradise—same as Abraham's bosom.

Christ's death on the cross is the dividing line of many Scriptural truths, including intermediate state of the dead.

~ Before the cross—men went below surface of earth to one of two compartments (Luke 16:19-31; Numbers 16:33; Matthew 12:40; Ephesians 4:9, 10; Philippians 2:9, 10).

~ At the time of the cross—Jesus went to Hades (Psalms 16:10), as did the thief on the cross (Luke 23:43b). Christ remained three days in Paradise of Hades in fellowship with pre-cross believers.

~ After the cross—Christ ascended into the presence of God in heaven (Ephesians 4:8) with the Old Testament believers and now resides in the presence of God. Hades is emptied of all the righteous; Paradise went to glory (2 Corinthians 5:8, 12:2-4).

In summary, we note concerning the intermediate state of the righteous that:

- The soul of the believer, at death, enters into the presence of Christ (2 Corinthians 5:1-8; Luke 23:43; John 14:3; 2 Timothy 4:18).

- That the intermediate state is greatly preferable to that of faithful and successful laborers for Christ here (Philemon 1:23).

- Departed believers are alive and conscious (Matthew 22:32; Luke 16:22, 23, 43; John 11:26; 1 Thessalonians 5:10; Romans 8:10; Philippians 1:6).

- Believers are at rest and blessed (Revelation 6:9-11, 14:13, 20:14).

These passages refute the idea of soul sleep during intermediate state (Acts 7:29; 1 Peter 3:19; 2 Corinthians 5:8).

In summary, we note concerning the intermediate state of the nonbeliever that:

- They are in prison, in torment and conscious suffering (Luke 16:23).

- They are under punishment (2 Peter 2:9).

These passages refute the view that suffering is purgatorial (Galatians 2:21; Hebrews 9:28; Romans 3:28; Luke 16:26; Hebrews 9:27; Revelation 22:11). At death the decision is made—there is no remedy from sin save by the blood of Christ.

IV. THE RAPTURE

First, we need a description of this present age, which in Galatians 1:4 is called "an evil age" because it is under the dominion of Satan (2 Corinthians 4:4), and is dark (Ephesians 6:12) and full of "ungodliness" and "lust" (Titus 2:12). It is different from other ages because:

- Christ was anticipated in other ages, but in this age He has come.

- The Holy Spirit resides in every believer; not so in previous ages.

❧ Revelation was not complete in previous ages; now it is— in Christ.

❧ Israel has been set aside; therefore, we do not expect God's promises to Israel to be completed in this age.

❧ More antagonism to God in this age than in others.

Purpose of Present Age

In Old Testament, God's dealing with Israel was as explained in His covenants; now, according to Acts 15:14, it is time for God to visit gentiles and "take out of them a people for His Name." This is the church (body, bride, temple, branch, flock, ministering priests, new creation, etc.), that in the ages to come He might show exceeding riches of His grace (Ephesians 2:7).

Description of Present Age

Mysterious (Colossians 1:24-27; Romans 16:25, 26; 1 Corinthians 2:7; Ephesians 3:5-9)—unrevealed until present age, although known by God from eternity.

Course of this present age described in:

❧ Matthew 13:
- ❧ Seed and soils—proclamation of kingdom.
- ❧ Wheat and darnell—imitation of kingdom.
- ❧ Mustard seed—extension of kingdom.
- ❧ Leaven—corruption of kingdom.
- ❧ Treasure—Israel during kingdom time.
- ❧ Pearl—church value revealed.
- ❧ Net—judgment at end of kingdom.

❧ Seven churches in Revelation 2, 3.

Definition of Rapture

Rapture is not a Scriptural word, but a Scriptural fact: It is the termination of the church age and the translation of the church into the presence of Christ and God with the Holy Spirit (John 14:1-3; 1 Thessalonians 4:13-18; 2 Thessalonians 2:1; 1 Corinthians

1:8, 15:51, 52; Philippians 3:20, 21; 2 Corinthians 5:1-19; Titus 2:13). It includes:

- ❧ The termination of the church age.
- ❧ The return of Christ for His bride.
- ❧ The resurrection of saints of the church age.
- ❧ The lifting from earth of living believers, who take on incorruptible bodies.
- ❧ The raising of the bodies of dead saints, whose bodies rejoin their disembodied souls and spirits and become incorruptible.
- ❧ The Tribulation begins with unbelievers who are left behind.
- ❧ It introduces end-time prophecies for Israel on the earth and church in heaven.

Premillennial schools are divided into a number of camps.

- ❧ Partial Rapturist—believe that only saints who are watching or waiting will be raptured (based on such passages as Philippians 3:20; Titus 2:13; 2 Timothy 4:8; Hebrews 9:28). We reject this theory because:
  - ❧ Christ's death frees sinner from condemnation and renders him acceptable to God.
  - ❧ Denies New Testament teaching on unity of body of Christ.
  - ❧ Denies completion of resurrection as described in 1 Corinthians 15:51, 52; 1 Thessalonians 4:14.
  - ❧ We're saved and taken by grace, not by works.
  - ❧ Denies distinction between Israel and church.
  - ❧ Places portion of church in Tribulation.

- ❧ Post-Tribulation Rapture theory—claims that Rapture takes place after the Tribulation. The post-Tribulation idea denies dispensation, distinctions between Israel and church; denies objectives of Tribulation, such as wrath, judgment, indignation, trial, etc.; views all verses on Second Coming as one event even though there would be definite contradictions; denies the doctrine of imminence and the historical fulfillments of passages such as Daniel 9:24-27; confuses Scripture passages concerning Israel and the church, such as Matthew 13, 24, 25; Revelation 2, 3, 4-19. Therefore, we reject this theory.

- Mid-Tribulation Rapture theory—teaches that the church will be raptured at the end of the first three and one-half years of the seventieth week of Daniel. The church will endure the events of the first half of the Tribulation, which to the mid-Tribulationist is not the manifestation of divine wrath. The Rapture is said to take place at the seventh trumpet and at the catching-up of two witnesses of Revelation 11. It is a compromise between pre- and post-Tribulation views. We reject this view because it:
  - Like the "post-Tribs," denies or weakens dispensationalism.
  - Denies distinctions between Israel and church.
  - Insists upon two separate and unrelated halves of Tribulation.
  - Denies doctrine of imminence.
  - Denies concept of church as a mystery and overlaps church's program with Israel's program.
  - Depends upon spiritualizing certain texts.
  - Rejects passages indicating that church is delivered from wrath.
  - Seventh trumpet is not a rapture, but rather a revelation of Christ in heaven as king during Millennium (not on earth, which comes later).

- Pre-Tribulation Rapture theory—holds that the entire body of Christ, the church, will by resurrection and translation be removed from earth before seventieth week of Daniel (Tribulation) begins. The pre-Tribulation Rapture theory rests on the literal method of interpretation of Scripture. This means that one who is a pre-Tribulationist also believes in a dispensational interpretation of God's Word. The church and Israel are two distinct groups with whom God works separately. The church age is a mystery, unrevealed in the Old Testament, and must be completed before God resumes and completes His program with Israel. We now summarize

Pentecost's "Essential Arguments of the Pre-Tribulation Rapturists" (in Pentecost, 1958):

- ⤙ It is the result of a literal method of interpretation. This is the basic issue between amillennialists and premillennialists. To be consistent, "Non-premills" must interpret Revelation and other passages as either historical (already happened in past) or spiritualize certain passages.
- ⤙ The seventieth week, according to both Old Testament and New Testament, is a period of:
  - ⤙ Wrath (Zephaniah 1:15, 18; 1 Thessalonians 1:9, 10; Revelation 6:16, 17, 11:18, 14:19, 15:1, 7, 16:1-19).
  - ⤙ Judgment (Revelation 14:8, 15:4, 16:5-7, 19:2).
  - ⤙ Indignation (Isaiah 26:20, 21, 34:1-3).
  - ⤙ Punishment (Isaiah 24:20, 21).
  - ⤙ Hour of trial (Revelation 3:10).
  - ⤙ Hour of trouble (Jeremiah 30:7).
  - ⤙ Destruction (Joel 1:15).
  - ⤙ Darkness (Joel 2:2; Zephaniah 1:14-18; Amos 5:18).

  These references describe the period in its entirety, not just the last half. It is truly a period of divine wrath.
- ⤙ The scope of the seventieth week—the whole earth (Revelation 3:10; Isaiah 34:2, 24:1, 4, 5, 16-21), yet while the whole earth is in view Israel is singled out particularly. Inasmuch as Ephesians 3:1-6 and Colossians 1:25-27 make it clear that the church is a mystery and its nature (composed of both Jew and gentile alike) was not revealed in the Old Testament, the church could not have been in view in this or any other Old Testament prophecy. The church is not in view in any major passage on the Tribulation, such as Matthew 24; Daniel 12; Luke 21; Mark 13; Jeremiah 30; or Revelation 7 on.
- ⤙ The purposes of the seventieth week:
  - ⤙ "To try them that dwell on the earth," but not the church (Revelation 3:10—read whole verse).
  - ⤙ To send Elijah to turn Israel back to God (Malachi 4:5, 6). Elijah's one ministry is to prepare the remnant in Israel for the advent of the Lord, even as stated in

Mark 9:12, 13, where John the Baptist acted in the capacity of the special ministry of Elijah.

- The unity of the seventieth week—though the week is divided into two parts in Daniel 9:27; Matthew 24:15; and Revelation 13, everywhere else the week is one and it is impossible to include church in the whole week and, consequently, in a part of the whole.

- The true church will be raptured, but the professing church will not—it will go into the Tribulation. This is true because the church is the body and Christ is the head (bride of the bridegroom, object of His love, etc.), and in Revelation 13:7 all in the Tribulation are brought into subjection to the beast, which would be impossible for those who are a part of Christ; that is, a part of the true church.

V. The Tribulation

When Christ was asked by His disciples when His Second Coming would occur and the age would end, Christ answered lengthily (Matthew 24). In 24:3-8, He listed some events between the first coming and the Rapture. The Rapture, I believe, takes place between verses 8, 9 and the first three and one-half years of Tribulation from verses 9-14, followed by the Great Tribulation (last three and one-half years) described in verses 15-26 and Christ's Second Coming in verses 27-31.

Scripture refers to at least three tribulations, which must be distinguished each from the other lest confusion arise:

1. The tribulation of the church.

2. The tribulation of Israel.

3. The Great Tribulation.

It is important that we take time here to distinguish between tribulation and the Great Tribulation. Much confusion has arisen because of the failure to distinguish between general suffering and the specific period of Great Tribulation described in the Old and New Testaments.

The Tribulation of the Church

The church (the body of Christ) is separate from Israel. Because the church is a part of Christ and separate from the world in its scope, goals, interests, and priorities, it will be looked upon in the world as a strange composition of people. Since the world lacks any inhibitions from the indwelling Spirit, it will attempt, out of jealousy, guilt, impatience, and lust, to set aside anything that would inhibit our sinful existence in this life. The church in its purity and eternal vision will be contrary to the world, and thus will become the target of the world's wrath: tribulation for the church. This is referred to in 1 Thessalonians 3:4 and prophesied in 2 Timothy 3:12. Satan, the hater of the church, directs persecution against it, and as each member suffers all suffer with it. Paul says as much in Colossians 1:24 (afflictions—Greek *thlipsis* means "tribulation"). John likewise mentions the tribulation he is undergoing as a believer in the church (Revelation 1:9). Note that this is not the Great Tribulation.

The Tribulation of Israel

Often called "Jacob's trouble" (Jeremiah 30:7). It lasts for seven years and is also known as the seventieth week of Daniel; it is for Israel and the unsaved world alone (Daniel 9:24-27). The church will not go through any part of this seven-year tribulation. This period is described in Revelation 6–19 and is identified when the beast confirms the covenant with the Jews. It is concluded with the revelation of Christ coming in judgment at Armageddon.

As early as Deuteronomy 4:29, 30, Israel is warned of this day, and Jeremiah brings it into sharper focus (Jeremiah 30:1-10). This period will begin with the making of a "firm covenant" between the coming Roman prince and the Jewish people. Note some of the aspects of this period.

The Political Aspect

    ✠ First, a period of the times of gentiles (Daniel 2:31-43; Luke 21:24) and the four beasts (Daniel 7:1-28; Revelation

13:1-10); the end of this sixty-nine weeks is described in Revelation 19:17-21.

- It will be a time of a federated political world, eventually dominated by ten cooperating kingdoms chiefly from the old Roman empire area. Different nations and powers will arise, challenge, and complement this Roman empire during the seven years:
  - "King of the north"—Russia through Syria.
  - "King of the east"—probably the hordes of the Orient, east of the Euphrates.
  - "King of the south"—African nations.
  - The "ecumenical church of the period" in the beginning but later destroyed.

- The ruler of this ten-federated-state group is referred to as the "beast out of the sea" in Revelation 13:1-10, where we see John changing the "horns" of Daniel into "crowns," as another time of great power has come. This ruler is a member of Satan's counterfeit trinity and will be the one who establishes a seven-year peace pact with Israel at the beginning of the "seventieth week" or time of "Jacob's trouble." This will seem to restore a semblance of order in the world for a very short time. In our studies, we refer to this political leader as the "beast" (Revelation 19:19, 20), rather than the antichrist as some do. We call the religious leader of the period the antichrist or "false prophet" (Revelation 19:20).

- It seems that during the first part of the Tribulation time, there will be a "vying for power" between nations of the earth, with the King of the north always threatening, while the multitudinous King of the east impatiently gathers arms and power in preparation to go to war against the world and the riches of the south seem to be a plum that many desire to pluck. The battles of the "seals," or the beginning part of the Tribulation, involve these nations as they compete for power.

- In the end we see the beast confront all of them in the latter part of Daniel 11. He breaks the covenant with Israel at three and one-half years and seems to establish his throne in Jerusalem when he desecrates the temple (Daniel 9:27, 12:11; Matthew 24:15; 2 Thessalonians 2:4). He commences to chase down and kill the Jews in a terrible holocaust, as well as fighting the other nations of the world while unifying them for the great climactic battle of Armageddon (Revelation 19), in which the forces of the earth unite against Christ and the host from Heaven on the plains of Megido in northern Israel. (Actually, "Armageddon" could refer to a series of final wars.)

> Christ will defeat the beast and world (Revelation 19:17-21) and introduce a time of judgments and rewards and establish the Millennial time when He shall sit upon the throne.

The Religious Aspect

> Scriptural citations (Revelation 13:11-18, 17:1-7).

> Jesus predicted that another would come in His own name and that the Jews would accept Him.

> The false church rides the beast (Revelation 17:7), and probably is one great federated apostate church united in a false religion. Finally, the effort to unite all churches into one great ecumenical church will succeed, but it will be a union of unbelievers. At the beginning of the Tribulation it will dominate the government, but in the midst of the period it seems that the beast will cast off this cumbersome church (Daniel 9:27; Revelation 17:16, 17), and establish a religion instituting worship of himself, the beast, and headed up by the false prophet, probably a Jew in Israel.

> This is the beast of Revelation 13:11-18, also called the "antichrist." This word appears in the New Testament five times in 1 and 2 John, but refers to the personal antichrist just once or twice; we think this term more accurately describes the "false prophet" or another member of the counterfeit trinity, probably a Jew who will lead many into the blasphemous worship of the beast. Sadly, Israel falls into

idolatry again for the final time just before they return to the Lord. From this time on (the last three and one-half years), all will be required to worship the beast and are led by the false prophet in so doing (Revelation 13:4, 6-8). He will use "deception" and "lying wonders" (Revelation 13:13) as well as force (Revelation 13:7, 15, 6:9-11, 20:4), persecution, and boycott (Revelation 13:16, 17), requiring all to take the mark of the beast. Multitudes will be slain for the Word of God and their testimony, but in the end Christ will destroy all.

The Israeliteish Aspect

- ✵ Scriptural citations (Ezekiel 37:1-28; Jeremiah 30:1-11; Daniel 12:1, 2, 9-13; Matthew 24:15-29, 32, 33; Revelation 7:1-8, 12:1-17, 14:1-5; Zechariah 12:8, 9, 14:1-9).

- ✵ The Jews are not wholly cast away; there is always a remnant according to election of grace (Romans 11:1-5).

- ✵ Finally, God will once again take up Israel as His people (Romans 11:29). This takes place during the Tribulation, when Israel, responding to God's judgment upon them through the hand of the God-hating gentiles of the Tribulation, returns to the Lord and becomes the testimony of His faithfulness and grace in this terrible period. They will become the missionaries, pastors, and witnesses of the Tribulation and lead many people of "every kindred, tongue and tribe" to God.

- ✵ Israel will return to Palestine during the beginning of the Tribulation and at the beginning of the Millennium: regathered in unbelief in the beginning, according to Ezekiel 37:7-10, and then to be restored to God later in that period (37:11-14). Evidently, just before the second half of the Tribulation, 144,000 Jews, as described in Revelation 7, will be converted and become the world's most effective missionaries.

- ✵ As a result of their stand for God, they will be hated, hunted, persecuted, and slain for the name of Christ.

ᴥ Satan will be cast out of heaven and in his hatred will persecute Israel by sending out armies to capture, torture, and kill them—but God uses the earth to protect Israel as described in the swallowing of the armies (Revelation 17:1-9; Daniel 12:1; Jeremiah 30:7).

ᴥ Israel will run to the mountains; the restored sacrifices in the temple of the first part of the Tribulation will be replaced by abolition of sacrifices. The beast will set up an image in the temple during the last three and one-half years, and the time of "abomination of desolation" (Daniel 12:11; Matthew 24:15; Revelation 13:14, 15) will take place. The slaying of the two great witnesses (Revelation 11) will trigger the last terrible days of holocaust for Israel, many of whom will have by then returned to the Lord. Some will survive and go on to great blessing during the Millennium, as will persons martyred during those days.

The Great Tribulation

According to Daniel 9:27, there will be a time in the midst of the last seven years when a definite turn for the worse will take place; it is signaled by the beast's breaking of his covenant with Israel. It will last 1,290 days which is 3½ years plus a few days (probably for the Second Coming of Christ and early judgments). It will end with the Second Coming of Christ (Daniel 7:13, 14) and establishment of the Millennium.

The Great Tribulation in Matthew 24:15-29 is described in that context. It is so severe that unless shortened (literally terminated), no human beings would survive. *Shortened* does not mean less than forty-two months, but rather terminated at Christ's coming; if He didn't come, humanity would exterminate itself.

Characteristics of that period include false prophets and christs (Matthew 24:23, 24); false reports of Christ's coming (24:26); and unnatural phenomena (24:29). Opinions vary as to whether Revelation 6-18 deal solely with the Great Tribulation or in part with the entire seven years, coming to more intense agony in the last three and one-half years. What is certain is that all the terrible events of the seals, trumpets, and vials of Revelation will be intensified in the last three and one-half years.

It appears that the sixth vial of Revelation is related to preparation for the great battle(s) of Armageddon. According to Revelation 16:14, armies gather to battle against the beast. Because of an illusion of Satan, they think they are fighting for world power, but in reality they are being gathered by Satan to oppose Christ and His armies in the final confrontation at Armageddon.

VI. SPECIFICS ON THE BEAST

The "beast" is apparently a gentile ruler. He is at the least the head of a block of ten gentile nations, who rises to prominence at the beginning of the Tribulation and continues to rise until he challenges the whole world—militarily and religiously—to follow him during the Tribulation time. His person and work are presented in Ezekiel 28:1-10; Daniel 7:7, 8, 20-26, 8:23-25, 9:26, 27, 11:36-45 (part or all); 2 Thessalonians 2:3-10; and Revelation 13:1-10, 17:8-14.

Details on His Person and Work

- He is often called the antichrist (1 John 2:18); also the "man of sin," as well as many other names throughout Scripture:
  - The Bloody and Deceitful Man (Psalms 5:6).
  - The Wicked One (Psalms 10:2-4).
  - The Man of the Earth (Psalms 10:18).
  - The Mighty Man (Psalms 52:1).
  - The Enemy (Psalms 55:3).
  - The Adversary (Psalms 74:8-10).
  - The Head of Many Countries (Psalms 111:6).
  - The Violent Man (Psalms 140:1).
  - The Assyrian (Isaiah 10:5-12).
  - The King of Babylon (Isaiah 14:2).
  - The Sun of the Morning (Isaiah 14:12).
  - The Spoiler (Isaiah 16:4, 5; Jeremiah 6:26).
  - The Nail (Isaiah 22:25).

- The Branch of the Terrible Ones (Isaiah 25:5).
- The Profane Wicked Prince of Israel (Ezekiel 21:25-27).
- The Little Horn (Daniel 7:8).
- The Prince that shall come (Daniel 9:26).
- The Vile Person (Daniel 11:21).
- The Willful King (Daniel 11:36).
- The Idol Shepherd (Zechariah 11:16, 17).
- The Man of Sin (2 Thessalonians 2:3).
- The Son of Perdition (2 Thessalonians 2:3).
- The Lawless One (2 Thessalonians 2:8).
- The Antichrist (1 John 22:22).
- The Angel of the Bottomless Pit (Revelation 9:11).
- The beast (Revelation 11:7, 13:1).

To these could be added: the One Coming in His Own Name (John 5:43), the King of Fierce Countenance (Daniel 8:23), the Abomination of Desolation (Matthew 24:15), the Desolator (Daniel 9:27). It is thus possible to see how extensive the revelation is concerning this individual. It is not surprising, as this one is Satan's great masterpiece in the imitation of the program of God.

Person

- Throughout history we see varied teachings concerning his person. Antiochus Epiphanes, during the time of the Maccabees, was and is thought by many to have been this person, and the early church thought Nero was the beast. In the eleventh century, the Waldenses, Hussites, and Wycliffites declared the Roman church to be the beast; later the Roman church named Napoleon, and even later Kaiser Wilhelm, Benito Mussolini, and Adolf Hitler were all touted as the beast. It is useless to speculate, because he will not be revealed until after the Rapture (2 Thessalonians 2:1-12).

- He is not a system or a church; he is a man (Revelation 13:18).

- He will commence his rule out of the nations of the revived Roman empire, possibly in Rome, but then will shift his throne to Jerusalem.

- He probably will be a Jew, though ruling gentile nations. Many also think that he will be a Syrian. A Jew by birth, a Roman by citizenship, and a Syrian by nationality is a possibility (Daniel 8:9).
  - "God of his fathers" means Abraham, Isaac, and Jacob (Daniel 11:37a).
  - "Another" implies another Jew (John 5:43).
  - Some Jews apparently will accept him as messiah. They would not accept a gentile as such.
- He will be a genius.
  - Intellectually (Daniel 8:23; Ezekiel 28:3).
  - Oratorically (Daniel 11:21b).
  - Governmentally—will rise from obscurity to great power (Daniel 7, 8: "little horn") and will receive all power from kings as beast of Revelation 13, 14.
  - Militarily—rider of white horse (Revelation 6:2, 13:4b).
  - Religiously (2 Thessalonians 2:4).
  - Commercially—no financial transactions without his seal (Revelation 13:17).
  - Financially (Daniel 11:43; Ezekiel 28:4, 5).

Scriptural Forerunners

- Coin (1 John 3:12).
- Nimrod—"mighty man against the Lord."
- Saul.
- Absalom—tried to steal kingdom by flattery and came to violent end.
- Nebuchadnezzar—first world ruler who typified last.

His Works and Goals

- To rule the world under the domination of Satan.
- To endeavor to destroy the Jew (Isaiah 10:12-27).
- He will rise to power after the Rapture by working out a seven-year peace treaty with Israel, which allows the

Israelites to rebuild the temple (impossible today), and recognizes them as a nation. He will have great power from Satan who, according to Revelation 13:3, 12, is seemingly able to restore a mortally wounded head—perhaps a strong ally, though some believe it is the beast himself.

- During the middle of the Tribulation, he will move to Jerusalem and have his image raised in the temple to be worshipped. He will then endeavor to destroy the Jews and rule the world.

- He will be spared by others of the world, but will be destroyed in the midst of plans and wars by Christ at His Second Coming, along with all the kings and armies of the earth.

Other Facts Concerning the Beast

These items are drawn from Pentecost (1958):

- He will appear on the scene in the "latter" times of Israel's history (Daniel 8:23).

- He will not appear until the Day of the Lord has begun (2 Thessalonians 2:2).

- His manifestation is being hindered by the Restrainer (2 Thessalonians 2:6, 7).

- This appearance will be preceded by a departure (2 Thessalonians 2:3), which may be interpreted either as a departure from the faith or a departure of the saints to be with the Lord (2 Thessalonians 2:1).

- He is a gentile. Because he arises from the sea (Revelation 13:1), and because the sea represents the gentile nations (Revelation 17:15), he must be of gentile origin.

- He rises from the Roman Empire, because he is a ruler of the people who destroyed Jerusalem (Daniel 9:26).

- He is the head of the last form of gentile world dominion, for he is like a leopard, a bear, and a lion (Revelation 13:1; *cf.* Daniel 7:7, 8, 20, 24; Revelation 17:9-11). As such, he is a political leader. The seven heads and ten horns (Revelation 13:1, 17:12) are federated under his authority.

- His influence is worldwide, for he rules over all nations (Revelation 17:12).

- He eliminates three rulers in his rise to power (Daniel 7:8, 24). One of the kingdoms over which he has authority has been revived, for one of the heads, representing a kingdom or king (Revelation 17:10), has been healed (Revelation 13:13).

- His rise comes through his peace program (Daniel 8:25).

- He is marked by his intelligence and persuasiveness (Daniel 7:8, 20, 8:23) and also by his subtlety and craft (Ezekiel 28:6), so that his position over the nations is by their own consent (Revelation 17:13).

- He rules over the nations in his federation with absolute authority (Daniel 11:36), and he is depicted as doing his own will. This authority is manifested through changes in laws and customs (Daniel 7:25).

- His chief interest is might and power (Daniel 11:38).

- As the head of the federated empire, he makes a seven-year covenant with Israel (Daniel 9:27), which is broken after three and one-half years (Daniel 9:27).

- He introduces idolatrous worship (Daniel 9:27) in which he sets himself up as god (Daniel 11:36, 37; 2 Thessalonians 2:4; Revelation 13:5).

- He is a blasphemer because of his assumption of deity (Ezekiel 28:2; Daniel 7:25; Revelation 13:1, 5, 6).

- He is energized by Satan and is controlled by the pride of the devil (Ezekiel 28:2; Daniel 8:25).

- He is the head of Satan's lawless system (2 Thessalonians 2:3); his claim to power and to deity are proved by signs wrought through satanic power (2 Thessalonians 2:9-19).

- He is received as god and as ruler because of the blindness of the people (2 Thessalonians 2:11).

- This ruler becomes the great adversary of Israel (Daniel 7:21, 25, 8:24; Revelation 13:7).

◦ There will come an alliance against him (Ezekiel 28:7; Daniel 11:40, 42), which will contest his authority.

◦ In the ensuing conflict, he will gain control over Palestine and adjacent territory (Daniel 11:42) and will make his headquarters in Jerusalem (Daniel 11:45).

◦ This ruler, at the time of his rise to power, is elevated through the instrumentality of the "harlot," the corrupt religious system, which consequently seeks to dominate him (Revelation 17:3).

◦ This religious system is destroyed by the beast-ruler so that he may rule unhindered (Revelation 17:16, 17).

◦ He becomes the special adversary of the Prince of Princes (Daniel 8:25), His program (2 Thessalonians 2:4; Revelation 17:14), and His people (Daniel 7:21, 25, 8:24; Revelation 17:7).

◦ Although he continues to wield power for seven years (Daniel 9:27), his satanic activity is confined to the last half of the Tribulation period (Daniel 7:25, 9:27, 11:36; Revelation 13:5).

◦ His rule will be terminated by a direct judgment from God (Ezekiel 28:6; Daniel 7:22, 26, 8:25, 9:27, 11:45; Revelation 19:19, 20). This judgment will take place as he is engaged in a military campaign in Palestine (Ezekiel 28:8, 9; Revelation 19:19), and he will be cast into the lake of fire (Revelation 19:20; Ezekiel 28:10).

◦ This judgment will take place at the second advent of Christ (2 Thessalonians 2:8; Daniel 7:22) and will constitute a manifestation of Christ's Messianic authority (Revelation 11:15).

◦ The kingdom over which the beast ruled will pass to the authority of the Messiah and will become the kingdom of the saints (Daniel 7:27).

VII. SPECIFICS ON THE FINAL RELIGIOUS LEADER— THE FALSE PROPHET

This second beast is most fully described in Revelation 13:11-17 and is most often referred to as "False Prophet." Pentecost (1958) lists some of the important factors concerning this false religious leader of the last times (especially the last three and one-half years of the Tribulation) as follows:

- ✒ This individual is evidently a Jew, since he arises out of the earth, or land, that is Palestine (13:11).

- ✒ He is influential in religious affairs (13:11: "two horns like a lamb").

- ✒ He is motivated by Satan, as is the first beast (13:11).

- ✒ He has delegated authority (13:13: "The power of the first beast").

- ✒ He promotes the worship of the first beast and compels the earth to worship the first beast as god (13:12).

- ✒ His ministry is authenticated by the signs and miracles that he does, apparently proving that he is Elijah who was to come (13:13, 14).

- ✒ He is successful in deceiving the unbelieving world (13:14).

- ✒ The worship promoted is an idolatrous worship (13:14, 15).

- ✒ The false prophet has the power of death to compel men to worship the beast (13:15).

- ✒ He has authority in the economic realm to control all commerce (13:16, 17).

- ✒ He has a mark that will establish his identity to those who live in that day (13:18).

This completes the "unholy trinity": this second beast, subservient to the first, acts as the beast's prophet or spokesman. The unholy trinity is the dragon (Satan), the beast, and the false prophet (Revelation 16:13). Satan endeavors to assume the place occupied by God, the Beast the place of Christ, and the False Prophet the place of the Holy Spirit.

VIII. ARMAGEDDON

A very difficult portion of God's final dealings with the satanic forces of the earth is the description of the Battle of Armageddon. We will endeavor, first, to describe what it is not; and secondly, what it is, with Scriptural references in both cases. There are many interpretations of this battle; here is ours.

What It Is Not

❦ It is not World Wars I and/or II.

❦ It is not the first battle of Gog and Magog, as described in Ezekiel 38-39.

❦ It is not the war in Heaven described in Revelation 12:7-17.

❦ It is not the battle fought after the Millennium when Satan is loosed for a season. This battle is sometimes called the second battle of Gog and Magog.

❦ It is not the battle between the Roman Empire and the Northern Confederacy (Syria, Russia/allies).

What It Is

We believe there will be a series of battles between existing powers of earth, all vying for power. The emerging power will be the Roman empire beast who, energized by Satan, in the middle of the Tribulation, will headquarter in Jerusalem and will prepare to battle the remaining armies of the earth at the end of the Tribulation. At that time there will be a spectacular sign from Heaven (Matthew 24:30), which will unite all of the remaining armies of the earth, together with the beast, to fight Christ and His army. Some details and chronology are herewith listed:

❦ We believe Armageddon is not an isolated battle, but rather a campaign that extends over the last three and one-half years of the Tribulation, with many battles. The Greek word *polemos* used in Revelation 16:14 means "war" or "campaign"; otherwise, *mache* would have been used to indicate a single battle.

๛ The northern confederacy will consist of Russia, Syria, Ethiopia, Libya, Germany, and Turkey (Ezekiel 38:2, 5, 6); this bloc will invade Israel and possibly the south for spoils (Ezekiel 38:11, 12; Daniel 11). We believe this is the red horse of war of Revelation 6:3, at the beginning of the seven years of Tribulation, because it takes seven years to clean up the debris (Ezekiel 39:9, 10).

๛ The Roman beast protests this invasion because of his treaty with Israel; he also brings forth a satanic imitation of the fulfillment of the Abrahamic Covenant, which gives Israel title deed to the land, but the warning goes unheeded.

๛ The northern confederacy (Russia and company) will be destroyed by God's intervention—a convulsion of nature (Ezekiel 38:20-22)—rather than by an opposing army.

๛ The Armageddon campaign is not located in just one place; rather, several locations are involved in this campaign, as described in Scripture. Obviously, a climactic battle with the final confrontation will take place on a plain in north central Palestine, ten miles south of Nazareth and fifteen miles in from the Mediterranean. This is Megiddo and the plain of Esdraelon, from whence the name *Armageddon* (Hill of Megiddo) is derived; it is the place of the confrontation between the forces of the beast and Christ and where the Tribulation is completed as the beast is defeated and cast into the lake of fire along with his followers and cohorts.

๛ Other areas of battle between final existing powers, leading up to the climax, include one in the Valley of Jehosophat, east of Jerusalem (Joel 3:2, 13). The Lord comes from Edom (Idomea), south of Jerusalem, after judgment (Isaiah 34, 63); this seems to be the first stop after His return. Jerusalem is also mentioned as a center of conflict (Zechariah 12:2-11, 14:2). In fact, Revelation speaks of blood up to horses' bridles for 1,600 furlongs or the whole length of Israel (Revelation 14:20).

๛ The participants in the battle include the Roman beast and his ten nations, the King of the East (Asiatic nations beyond the Euphrates), the King of the South (Northern African nations), and possibly whatever is left of the northern confederacy after God's destruction of its army by nature. These will be ranged against Christ and His heavenly followers.

- ✺ Results of the final battle of the Armageddon campaign:
  - ✦ The armies of the beast and the East are destroyed by Christ. (The northern army was destroyed earlier by God, in a supernatural event, and the southern army was destroyed by the beast, also earlier).
  - ✦ The beast and false prophet are cast into the lake of fire (Revelation 19:20).
  - ✦ Satan is bound (Revelation 30:2).
  - ✦ Christ initiates the final judgments of Revelation 20 and proceeds to set up His kingdom for a Millennial reign.

IX. THE SECOND COMING OF CHRIST

We must remember that we are studying these last-time themes in order to establish the fact that there is a Scriptural goal. The themes of the Second Coming, Armageddon, satanic control of government during the Tribulation, as well as the final judgments and resurrections, are all a part of correct interpretation of the Bible.

The Second Coming of Christ occurs in two phases: the coming of Christ *for* His saints, as described in the section on the Rapture, which took place before the Tribulation; and the coming of Christ *with* His saints after the Tribulation. This latter coming will set into work the final judgments, Millennium, etc. It is the grand climax of the program of God.

The Second Coming of Christ is the major theme of Old Testament prophecy, as it is the very center of the covenants with Abraham, Israel, and David. It is also the central theme of all prophetic books. The Second Coming of Christ is important! It is the first prophecy uttered by man (Jude 1:14, 15), the last message of the ascended Christ, and the last word of the Bible (Revelation 22:20, 21). It occupies more of the text of Scripture than any other doctrine—so let's study this vigorously. First we will look at views of the Second Advent, followed by scrutiny of the Old Testament prophecies of the Second Coming, New Testament prophecies of the Second Coming, and practical exhortations for us from the truth of the Second Coming.

Views of the Second Advent

Postmillennial View

- Especially popular among covenant theologians and during the Dark Ages.

- Teaches that the whole world will eventually be Christianized before the coming of Christ. The world will become better and better until His return.

- Advocates believe in a literal return and Millennium, and usually follow the Old Testament teaching as to the description of the Millennial kingdom.

- There is dispute over the initiation of the kingdom (when Christ will return) in relation to Millennium, and over what He will do.

Amillennial View

- Teaches that there will be no literal Millennium on the earth following the Second Advent; holds that all prophecies concerning the kingdom are being fulfilled now, spiritually, by the church.

- Denies the literal reign of Christ on earth; argues that Satan has been bound since the birth of Christ and that the church age *is* the Millennium.

Premillennial View (which We Hold)

- Teaches that Christ will return to earth literally and bodily to establish a Millennial kingdom.

ॐ He will reign over that kingdom and all covenants (promises) given to Israel will be literally fulfilled.

ॐ His kingdom will continue for 1,000 years, after which it will be merged into the eternal state of God's plan for believers.

A brief history of premillennialism includes the following facts:

ॐ Early church was solidly premillennial from the apostolic era on.

ॐ The union of church and state under Constantine was a death knell to premillennialism, as it then looked as though Christianity would rise to influence the world politically.

ॐ Then arose Augustine, the greatest influencer of theology between Paul and the Reformation. He systematized Roman theology with an amillennialist approach; premillennial teaching went underground as Roman Catholic theology predominated the world. Augustine's *City of God* presented the visible church as the kingdom of God on earth. This work was one of the most influential books for hundreds of years.

ॐ The reformers emphasized salvation (soteriology) and did not deal much with eschatology. However, they did set a precedent or trend of a literal method of interpreting Scripture, which later led to the revival of premillennialism and the birth of dispensationalism.

ॐ The Brethren movement, which arose in England and Ireland around 1830, and the influence of John Darby (1800–1882) brought dispensationalism and premillennial teaching into prominence; these doctrines remain very strong today. The Brethren movement taught:

- ॐ That Christ's return is premillennial.
- ॐ That Christ's return is literal.
- ॐ That Christ's return is necessary to complete promises and fulfill prophecy.

Old Testament Prophecies of the Second Coming

- First clear prophecy concerning Christ's Second Coming is Deuteronomy 30:1-3: "Will return."

- Psalms frequently refer to return of Christ (Psalms 1, 2, 24, 50, 72, 89, 96, 110).

- The major and minor prophets frequently refer to Second Coming (e.g., Isaiah 9:6, 7, 11, 12, 63:1-6; Daniel 7:14; Zechariah 2:10, 11, 8:3-8, 14:1-4).

New Testament Prophecies of the Second Coming

The New Testament adds a new facet to our knowledge of the Second Coming. In the Old Testament, the differences in certain passages were often obscured by the facts of the First Coming of Christ, but Rapture, the New Testament mystery, was never referred to. In the New Testament, the First Advent is past and the Rapture is introduced. We must be careful not to confuse those passages dealing with the Rapture and Christ's coming to earth to reign.

The New Testament contains at least twenty major passages dealing with revelation on this subject (one out of every twenty-five verses). Some of these are: Matthew 19:28, 23:39, 24:3-25; Mark 13:24-37; Luke 12:35-48, 17:22-37, 18:8, 21:25-28; Acts 1:10, 11, 156-18; Romans 11:25-27; 1 Corinthians 11:26; 2 Thessalonians 1:7-10; 2 Peter 3:3, 4; Jude 14, 15; Revelation 1:7, 8, 2:25-28, 16:15, 19:11-21, 22:20. These passages and others point out that the:

- Second Coming is post-Tribulational and premillennial.

- Second Coming is personal.

- Second Coming is visible and glorious.

- Second Coming is related to earth (to reign on earth).

- Second Coming is attended by angels and saints of heaven.

- Second Coming is to judge earth.

- Second Coming is to deliver the surviving martyrs of the Tribulation, both Jew and gentile.

- Second Coming introduces the Millennium and establishes the Davidic kingdom.

- Second Coming is to raise up David as prince over Israel, to rule over Old Testament saints (Ezekiel 37:24).

Practical Teachings from the Truth of the Doctrine of Second Advent

In *Things to Come*, Pentecost describes the following teachings and lessons, along with many others (1958, p. 394):

- Watchfulness (Matthew 24:42-44, 25:13; Mark 13:32-37; Luke 12:35-38; Revelation 16:15).

- Sobriety (1 Thessalonians 5:2-6; 1 Peter 1:13, 4:7, 5:8).

- Repentance (Acts 3:19-21; Revelation 3:3).

- Fidelity (Matthew 25:19-21; Luke 12:42-44, 19:12, 13).

- To be unashamed of Christ (Mark 8:38).

- Against worldliness (Matthew 16:26, 27).

- Moderation (Philemon 4:5).

X. THE RESURRECTIONS

Scripture teaches that there will be multiple resurrections. However, not all people, wicked and righteous, will be resurrected simultaneously. In fact, we find at least seven resurrections in Scripture, some past and some to come. Certain is the fact that human existence goes on forever. The seven resurrections are:

1. Resurrection of Christ—The first, or "first fruits," as argued in 1 Corinthians 15 in such beautiful detail. It is prophesied in the Old Testament in Psalms 16:9, 10, etc.; narrated in the Gospels; and supported theologically throughout the New Testament.

2. Resurrection of the saints in Jerusalem (Matthew 27:52, 53)—These were not raised until Christ, the "first fruit," was raised. Lazarus and others were resuscitated and died again;

those resurrected do not physically die again. These were probably a small group of Jerusalem saints who were caught up to heaven when their mission was accomplished.

3. Resurrection of church at the Rapture (1 Thessalonians 4:13-18; 1 Corinthians 15:51-58)—Saints will receive bodies like Christ (1 John 3:2).

4. Resurrection of Old Testament saints at end of Tribulation, the beginning of the Millennium (Daniel 12; Isaiah 26:19-21)—This completes the Jewish dispensation. Raised saints of the New Testament are "in Christ" (1 Thessalonians 4:16).

5. Resurrection of Tribulation saints—Possibly same as above, or possibly separated by a very short space of time (Revelation 20:4). "First resurrection" refers to all resurrections of saints, although some phases were separated by time. "Second resurrection" refers to resurrection of wicked (Revelation 20:5).

6. Resurrection of Millennial saints—Though it seems (Isaiah 65:20) that life is greatly lengthened, it appears that death will still come until the new heavens and earth come into existence. Death may be a form of judgment during that time. Chafer believes in a Millennial Rapture, as explained in *Major Bible Themes* (Chafer, 1974, p. 342).

7. Resurrection of the wicked (Revelation 20:11-15)—Great White Throne Judgment. The bodies received in this resurrection will be subject to pain and suffering (Daniel 12:2). This is what behooves believers to carry to the Gospel to lost men.

XI. JUDGMENTS OF THE END TIME

There are at least seven judgments related to end-time events:

1. Judgment of the church or believers concerning service (2 Corinthians 5:10; Revelation 22:12):

    ఌ Participants—believers.

- Time and location—immediately after Rapture, in heaven during Tribulation at judgment seat of Christ.

- Crowns that a believer may achieve.
  - Crown of life—reward for faithfulness (James 1:12).
  - Incorruptible crown—for those who live separated lives unto the Lord (1 Corinthians 9:25).
  - Crown of rejoicing—soul winners' crown (1 Thessalonians 2:19).
  - "Crown of glory"—shepherds', pastors' reward (1 Peter 5:2-4).
  - Crown of righteousness—for those who look forward to His coming (2 Timothy 4:8).

- Part of the reward will be to reign with Christ during the Millennium even as Israelites will (see later in this section). This will be done as in the time of Esther, when she reigned as bride and Mordecai as prime minister. Each has own respective duties.

2. Judgment of resurrected Israel and Tribulation saints (Revelation 20:4; Daniel 12:2; Isaiah 26:19):

   - Time and location—at return of Christ, apparently in Israel, as they will live and reign with Him for 1,000 years.

   - Participants—believing Israelites of previous generations and martyrs of Tribulation.

   - Basis—reward for their faithfulness in accepting and living for Christ.

3. Judgment of living Israel at return of Christ (Ezekiel 20:33-38; Malachi 3:2-5; Romans 9:6; Matthew 25:1-30):

   - Time and location—Tribulation is God's judgment on Israel with climax at end. Judgment will take place on earth.

   - Participants—all Israelites living at return of Christ; they will be regathered.

   - Basis of judgment—individual heart's attitude toward God.

4. Judgment of the gentiles (Matthew 25:31-46; Psalms 2; Isaiah 63:1-6; Joel 3:1, 2, 12; Zephaniah 3:8; Zechariah 14:1-19):

   ❧ Often called "nations"—*ta ethoe* in Greek of Matthew 25 is really better translated as "people." In truth, we have, in no age, seen whole nations accept a message and justify eternal salvation.

   ❧ Time and place—when Christ returns and judgment will take place on earth.

   ❧ Participants—living gentiles at end of Tribulation.

   ❧ Basis of judgment—treatment of brethren (Jews) who were under fearful persecution by government edict. To help them jeopardized own lives and portrayed faith in Christ and the brethrens' message of the coming kingdom.

5. Judgment of the wicked dead at the Great White Throne (Revelation 20:5, 11-15):

   ❧ Time and place—time is after the Millennium, probably some place between heaven and earth (Revelation 20:11).

   ❧ Participants—those who have rejected Christ; they are unsaved.

   ❧ Basis of judgment—whether the individual accepted Christ. "According to their works" indicates that these individuals refused to accept the work of Christ on Calvary in faith, opting instead to present their own works and righteousness to God; this is, of course, totally unacceptable. Sentence passed is the "second death" or separation from God forever in the "lake of fire."

6. Judgment of fallen angels, beast, and false prophet (witness), and of the devil and his angels. Possibly one, but probably two or more scenes of judgment:

   ❧ Fallen angels (Jude 6; 2 Peter 2:4). Satan and followers— cast to earth (Revelation 12:7-9, 13-17); bound in pit (Revelation 20:1-3) and judged (Revelation 20:9, 10).

Beast and his armies will be judged in defeat prior to this (Revelation 19:19-21; 2 Thessalonians. 2:8), but will probably be finally judged in the Revelation 20:9-10 scene.

- ❧ Time and place—end of Millennium, some place between heaven and earth.

- ❧ Participants—Satan, his angels, and probably all his followers.

- ❧ Basis of judgment—rejection of God's authority.

XII. THE GLORIOUS AGE OF THE MILLENNIUM

The Millennium is the 1,000-year reign of Christ which commences at the time of His Second Advent. There are three existing views of the Millennium.

Postmillennial View

Those who hold to a postmillennial view feel that there will be constant earthly improvement by governments of the earth, or a turning to God through some true church, which eventually will usher in a golden age of which the coming of Christ will be the climax.

Amillennial View

Spiritualizes passages regarding the kingdom of God. It says these things happen in the believer's heart or that the passages refer to the eternal state or present experience of the church on earth. Christ's return signals commencement of the eternal state.

Premillennialist View

We hold the premillennialist view, which accepts Scripture literally and believes that Christ will return with His resurrected saints to establish a golden 1,000-year period on earth with Christ reigning.

Description of the Millennial Reign of Christ on Earth

- Christ will return to the earth and establish a glorious earthly kingdom that will last for 1,000 years:
  - Old Testament (Deuteronomy 30:2-6 [first Old Testament prophecy on this subject]; Psalms 2, 24, 50, 72, 96, 110; Isaiah 9:6, 7, 11:1–12:6, 65, 66; Zechariah 14:3-11).
  - New Testament (Romans 11:25-27; 2 Thessalonians 1:7-10; 2 Peter 3:3, 4; Revelation 1:7, 8, 2:25-28, 19:11-21; many others).
  - The return will be personal, visible, glorious, and bodily. Geographically centered in vicinity of Jerusalem (Zechariah 14:1-21).
  - He will be accompanied by holy angels and resurrected saints (Matthew 25:31; 1 Thessalonians 3:13; Jude; Revelation 19:11-21).
- Purpose of return:
  - To judge the earth (Matthew 24:27-31, 46; 2 Thessalonians 1:7-9).
  - To deliver the elect out of the Tribulation time (Matthew 24:22; Romans 11:26, 27).
  - To reestablish Davidic kingdom (Amos 9:11, 12; Ezekiel 37:26; Luke 1:31-33).

Description of the Millennial Government

- Christ will reign (Psalms 2:8).
- It will be a righteous government (Isaiah 11; 42:4).
- Resurrected David will assist as a regent (Jeremiah 30:9, 33:15-17; Ezekiel 34:23, 24; Hosea 3:5).
- It will rule the entire earth (Daniel 2:35, 7:14, 27).
- It will be absolute in authority (Psalms 72:9-11; Isaiah 11:4).

Subjects of Millennial Age

- Believers out of the Tribulation, both gentile and Jew. Wicked will be put to death (Matthew 25:31-46; Ezekiel

20:33-38); parables of wheat and tares (Matthew 13:30, 31) and fish (Matthew 13:49, 50; Isaiah 65:11–66:16; Jeremiah 25:30-33).

- Israel is in prominence and blessing and will inhabit restored Jerusalem and Palestine (Isaiah 9:6, 7, 33:17, 22, 44:6; Jeremiah 23:5; Micah 2:13; etc.). Dwight Pentecost (1958) summarizes Israel's place thus:
  - They'll be converted and restored.
  - They'll be reunited as a nation (Jeremiah 3:18, 33:14; etc.).
  - They'll be exalted above gentiles (Isaiah 14:1, 2, 49:22, 23, 60:14-17, 61:6, 7).
  - They'll again be related to Jehovah by marriage (Isaiah 54:1-17, 62:2-5).
  - They'll be righteous (Isaiah 1:25, 2:4, 44:22-24; 35).
  - They'll be God's witnesses during Millennium (Isaiah 44:8, 21, etc.).
  - They'll be beautified to bring glory to Jehovah (Isaiah 62:3; Jeremiah 32:41; Hosea 14:5, 6, etc.).

- Gentiles, in lesser role, will be greatly blessed also (Isaiah 2:4, 11:12, 16:1-5; Jeremiah 3:17, 16:19).

- Later children born to those believers ushered in Millennial reign. These children will be subject to Christ's reign, and if openly rebellious they will be put to death (Isaiah 66:20, 24; Zechariah 14:16-19).

- Resurrected believers of all ages (immortal beings) will be subjects and co-rulers with Christ. This is one of the great arguments of amillennialists, who think it is facetious or ridiculous to have a civilization composed of humans who are mortal and resurrected believers who are immortal.
  - They forget the perfect harmony of the resurrected Savior, who came back to fellowship with the apostles and spoke, ate, walked, etc.
  - They also forget that Christ, who reigns, will be immortal.

Scripture appears to teach that we shall live apart in the new Jerusalem in a special world. We should be careful not to confuse promises given to the last earthly-generation saints (out of Tribulation) with those made to previous-generation saints.

❧ Hebrews 11:10; 13-16 obviously refers to a heavenly city for Old Testament saints, and Hebrews 12:22-24 refers to one for Christians of this age. Therefore, saints of all ages are included in the plans for new Jerusalem (Revelation 21:2, 9, 10).

❧ Some think that this heavenly Jerusalem is in existence during the Millennium and is hovering above earth as the habitation of resurrected saints. This explains references to nations and kings (Revelation 21:24), which some think are incongruous or incompatible with eternal state and, also, healing of nations (Revelation 22:2-4). The heavenly Jerusalem apparently is withdrawn at time of destruction of present heaven and earth; then, as described in Revelation 21:2, it returns to the new heaven and earth; this is described in Revelation 21:9, 10. Also Galatians 4:26 and Revelation 3:12 seem to refer to same city as Revelation 21:2, 10.

❧ If this is so—and it seems to be consistent with Scripture— then Millennial saints, it is to be assumed, will be transferred to the heavenly Jerusalem at the end of the Millennium. No Scripture for this, although John 14:2 seems to identify with Hebrews 12:23.

❧ We do know that resurrected saints will be involved in the Millennial government, with Christ, in judging (Matthew 19:28; 1 Corinthians 6:2) and reigning (Revelation 20:6, 5:10; 2 Timothy 2:12). This would, of course, require at least some amount of communication between Millennial citizens and resurrected saints.

General Characteristics of the Millennium

SOCIAL AND ECONOMIC CONDITIONS:

❧ Justice—complete and universal (Psalms 72; Isaiah 11).

❧ Peace.

❧ Most men are believers because enemies were eliminated at beginning.

- Curse of the earth lifted—good crops and less work (Isaiah 35:1, 2).
- Health, healing, and longevity (Isaiah 33:24, 29:18, 65:20).

PHYSICAL CHANGES:

- Palestine embraces all land promised to Abraham (Genesis 15:18-21).
- Jerusalem raised up and center of government and river will shoot forth out of temple to Dead Sea and Mediterranean (Zechariah 14:8); Dead Sea will be healed (Ezekiel 47:1-12).
- Mount Olive will split (Zechariah 14).

SPIRITUAL CHARACTERISTICS:

- Christ will reign in great power and glory (1 Peter 1:10, 11; Isaiah 40:4, 5).
- Truth over whole earth (Isaiah 11:9).
- Righteousness (Isaiah 11:3-5); peace (Isaiah 2:4); joy (Isaiah 12:3, 4); power of Spirit on earth (Isaiah 32:15; Joel 2:28, 29).
- A Millennial temple where is a throne and Christ rules, from which a river comes forth. Reestablishment of sacrifices that are not expiatory (Hebrews 9:26), but rather memorial, as is our Lord's Supper, which ends when He comes again (1 Corinthians 11: "'til He comes"). What a meaning these sacrifices will have!

Close of the Millennial State

- Satan will be loosed; human professors, who are not believers, will be deceived and join forces in rebellion (Revelation 20:7-9).
- Judgment of Satan (Revelation 20:10).
- Judgment of rebels and rejecters of all ages (Revelation 20:11-15). This, which is the reason for the Millennium, brings the Millennium to an end. Even though men, during the Millennium as in Eden, have a perfect environment

under a perfect ruler, they will fail, as men always do; every inhabitant of the eternal heaven is there by the grace of God.

✦ Finally comes the eternal state of Revelation 21, 22.

XIII. THE LAST STATE OF THE WICKED

The fate of the wicked is a very somber subject, in contrast to the joy we experience when we think and speak of our future as believers. We refer sadly to the final state of the unbelievers. To neglect this teaching is to neglect or censor portions of the Word itself, even the very words of Christ who preached with great authority on the state of the wicked dead.

Proposed Theories of the State of Wicked Dead

✦ Universalism—Argues that a God of love will not permanently send anyone to eternal punishment; many forms of universalism advocate the belief that all will be forgiven and saved and restored to God. This even includes the devil and his followers. We reject this on the basis of Acts 3:21-23; Matthew 18:9; John 3:36.

✦ Conditionalism—To accept Christ is eternal life; to reject means to die or go into a nonexistent state. This, of course, is pure speculation.

✦ Everlasting punishment—The Biblical teaching bases punishment on rejection of God's provision for the payment of sin: namely, Christ's death on the cross.
  ✦ Scriptural teaching concerning everlasting punishment.
    ✦ There will be a day of judgment (Acts 17:30, 31).
    ✦ Every man will be judged (Romans 2:5, 6; Revelation 20:12).
    ✦ Punishment is eternal (Mark 9:43-48).
    ✦ There will be degrees of punishment (Romans 2:5, 6; Revelation 20:12).
    ✦ There will be resurrection of the unjust as well as the just (John 5:29).

- ✤ It is referred to numerous times in Scripture (e.g., Matthew 25:46; Mark 9:45-48; John 3:36).
- ✤ Terms used to describe places of everlasting punishment.
  - ✤ Sheol—Hebrew word of Old Testament describing intermediate state.
  - ✤ Hades—Greek word of New Testament describing intermediate state.
  - ✤ Tartarus—wicked angels "who left their first estate" are chained there in darkness (2 Peter 2:4).
  - ✤ Gehenna—a word used by Christ to designate the eternal lake of fire; also the name of the garbage pit outside of Jerusalem that burned continuously.
  - ✤ Tophet—Old Testament word for lake of fire.
  - ✤ Abyss—place of fallen angels; not for human beings (Romans 10:7).
  - ✤ Lake of fire—final state; hell and its occupants are cast therein. Same as Gehenna and Tophet.

XIV. AFTER THE MILLENNIUM

Revelation 20:7-9 tells us of special happenings after the Millennium. This passage is unique and describes events that are not mentioned elsewhere in Scripture. The events happen in this order:

1. Satan is loosed for a short time; he has not learned, for he makes one last attempt to unseat God from His glory.

2. Nations deceived again by Satan and gathered to fight against God. Question: Who would follow Satan? Probably those born in the last years of the Millennium, who have not yet learned or accepted the magnificent grace of Christ as He rules. Salvation even in the Millennium depends on acceptance of Christ as Savior; the progeny of the Millennium are born with a sin nature, even as we are, and have to accept Christ even as we did. Satan's followers are rejecters.

XV. Eternal Final State of the Believers

God is careful to give us just enough information concerning our eternal state so that we, as believers, don't go committing suicide. He is faithful to let us know that He has stupendous plans for us in fellowship with Him for all of the eternities.

We have already studied some of the transitory happenings between the Rapture and the final state. We have examined the Rapture, Tribulation, Millennium, judgments, rewards, etc.; Revelation 20 describes the end of the Millennium, the last war of Satan against God, and his final assignment to the lake of fire with his angels. Now we come to the blessed teachings concerning the eternal state of the believer. Now we look into the preparation and commencement of the eternal kingdom.

Preparation for the eternal state includes:

- A purging of Satan (Revelation 20:2, 3, 7-10).

- A purging of rebellious humans, who have been rejecting since the sin of Adam (Revelation 20:11-15).

- A purging of the old earth and heavens (Matthew 5:18, 24, 34, 35; Mark 13:30, 31; 2 Peter 3:10; Revelation 21:1).
  - Note that the original word *parerchomai* is a verb of wide and general meaning such as "to go," "to come," "pass," etc. It does *not* mean annihilation. The main idea is transition.
  - This is consistent with the many passages that refer to the earth abiding forever (Ecclesiastes 1:4; Psalms 104:5, 119:90).

The New Heaven and New Earth

The briefest mention of the new heaven and new earth, in Revelation 21:1, is nowhere explained, although the new heaven and earth are referred to in Isaiah 65:17, 66:22 and 2 Peter 3:10-13. God has evidently chosen to keep silent on the attributes of the new heaven and earth because our finite minds weren't ready for the blessings set aside for us. We get a hint of that in passages like Romans 11:33, Ephesians 2:6-9, and Isaiah 64:4, which is quoted by Paul in 1 Corinthians 2:9.

The New Jerusalem—
The Eternal City (Revelation 21:1–22:7)

- It is a literal city, which must be distinguished from the new heavens and earth. It is represented as coming down out of heaven (Revelation 21:2), even though the kings of the earth bring their glory into it (21:24).

- Characteristics and descriptions:
  - It is a cube or pyramid that is 1,500 miles (12,000 furlongs) high, wide, and long. A literal golden city with foundations, walls, gates, etc.
  - God's glory provides the light (21:11, 23); consequently, no need for sun, moon, or stars. No night because God's glory is always there (21:25).
  - Its streets are gold, foundations garnished with precious stones. The wall is twenty stories high and made with jasper; the twelve huge gates bear the names of the twelve tribes of Israel, while the twelve foundations bear the names of the apostles.
  - The gates are huge pearls; they are never closed and are attended by twelve angels, three on each side.
  - A river of life flows from the throne of God within the city; the tree of life also is there, which constantly bears "twelve manner of fruit."

- The inhabitants are:
  - God the Father, Son, and Holy Spirit. We know this because:
    - "Behold the tabernacle of God is with men" (Revelation 21:1, 2).
    - This city has the glory of God (Revelation 21:11, 23, 22:5).
    - It has the throne of God and that service (22:3).
    - They shall see His face (22:4).
    - Lord God gives light to reign forever (22:5).
    - Also, John 14:2, 3 and Hebrews 13:14 teach of God's plan for a continuing city for Himself and His followers.
  - The Lamb's wife, the bride which is the church (Revelation 21:9, 10; John 14:2).

- Old Testament saints (Hebrews 11:10; Galatians 4:26; Hebrews 12:22, 23).
- Unfallen angels (Hebrews 12:22).

Meaning of Revelation 21:9–22:7

Does Revelation 21:9–22:7 describe the eternal state or the Millennial Jerusalem? Three views are presented here, with strong advocates for each view.

1. It describes the Millennium because:

    - Nations are mentioned in 22:2 and it refers to "healing of the nations." Are there sick nations in eternity? Those who oppose this view point out that words could be translated "for the health of the nations."

    - The existence of nations is proven because they (nations) enter "into" the new Jerusalem; thus, in earthly situation. *Answer*: Word should be "unto"; also, nation of Israel is referred to throughout eternity; why not others in relation to them (John 21:24-26)?

    - The nations walk in the light of Jerusalem (21:24). How can nations on earth be lighted if there is no earth or nations? Consequently, this city is Millennial, not eternal.

2. This city is eternal and describes the eternal state because:

    - Adjective "new" used in Revelation 21:1, 2.

    - Position of city; evidently suspended over earth (21:10).

    - God will reign from earthly Jerusalem, not heavenly (Zechariah 14:4). Since city is not on earth, how can Christ live therein and rule?

    - Characteristics of city are eternal, not Millennial:
        - "Glory of God."
        - No temple.
        - No light—there will be day and night in Millennium.
        - Throne of God is there.
        - No curse; effect of Fall removed.

‑❖ Tree of life, river of life, etc.

‑❖ Length of reign (Revelation 22:5).

3. This city is eternal, but moves its locale from its present place in heaven to a place above the earth during the Millennium, and then to its permanent place when the new heavens and earth are created by God. This is our view—we believe this because:

➣❖ It is a literal city to which Christ takes His bride after the marriage feast. The Rapture changes the saints' bodies into eternal, incorruptible bodies like His, and Christ will usher His bride into the place prepared for her (John 14:1-6; Revelation 21:9). It will also have within its confines saints of other ages (resurrected at the end of the Tribulation) (Hebrews 13:14).

➣❖ The city does exist during the Millennial age and it seems foolish to imply that it will be left unoccupied during the Millennium while resurrected saints live on the earth. Thus we see that God moves the habitation of the saints out of heaven to a place above the earth (Revelation 21:2), which casts its light upon the earth (21:24). This, then, is the dwelling place of all saints, old and new, during the Millennium.

➣❖ The saints will reside in the new Jerusalem but will reign with Him from that city, both church (Revelation 3:21) and Old Testament saints (Revelation 20:4). We find no restriction in Scripture to keep believers from coming and going at will, for it must be concluded that the resurrected saints of all ages in the city will be in their eternal state from their resurrection on, even though the earth during the Millennium will not have eternal blessings yet.

➣❖ Though the inhabitants of the city undergo no change, the locale of the city does; it descends once at the beginning of the Millennium, and then rises while the earth and heavens are purged and renovated by God. It descends a second time at the commencement of the eternal state, to act as the capital city of the new heavens and new earth.

The mistake lies in trying to make the new Jerusalem either a Millennial city *or* an eternal city. It is really both.

CONCLUSION

Let's always remember that the emphasis in all of these blessed teachings is on God and His glory, not in our future pleasant and blessed state. Our true happiness will come not because of perfect environment, but because of perfect fellowship with our Lord who is everything.

GRACE ACRES PRESS products and services bring joy to your heart and life. Visit us at www.GraceAcresPress.com

For orders or information about quantity discounts or reprints,
Call 888-700-GRACE (4722)
Fax (303) 681-9996
Email info@GraceAcresPress.com

CULTIVATING JOY

OTHER BOOKS YOU'LL ENJOY

The Intimate Warrior Series by Dave Wager

Beyond the Resistance:
 Learning to Face Adversity

Beyond the Compass:
 Learning to See the Unseen

Beyond the Deception:
 Learning to Defend the Truth

Beyond the Expectation:
 Learning to Obey

Beyond the Feeling:
 Learning to Listen

A Dad Beyond Measure
by Veronica Johnson